Naviga

a newcomer's guide

Sara Hopkinson

fernhurst
B O O K S

www.fernhurstbooks.co.uk

© Fernhurst Books 2006
First Published 2006 by
Fernhurst Books,
Duke's Path, High Street, Arundel,
West Sussex, BN18 9AJ, UK

Charts © Crown Copyright and/or database
rights. Reproduced by permission of the
Controller of Her Majesty's Stationery
Office and the UK Hydrographic Office
(www.ukho.gov.uk).

British Library Cataloguing in
Publication Data.
A catalogue record for this book is
available from the British Library.

ISBN 1 904475 18 3

Printed in China through World Print.

Artwork by Creative Byte.
Cover design by Balley Design.

Photographs of chartwork by Simon Davison.

Acknowledgements
The author would like to thank Roger
Seymour and Robin Cole (of Precision
Navigation) for their advice.

The publisher would like to thank
RAYMARINE for their help and generosity in
the preparation of this book. Also the United
Kingdom Hydrographic Office for their
permission to reproduce charts. In addition:
The Turkish Hydrographic Office (Seyir
Hidrografi ve Osinografi) for permission
to reproduce chart 1665; The Service
Hydrographique et Oceanographique de la
Marine for permission to reproduce chart
SC5602.1; Tim Davison photo page 79 and
cover photos. Pages 76-7 contain an extract
from a leaflet produced by the Maritime and
Coastguard Agency, for which many thanks.

* RYA and Yachtmaster are registered trademarks
of the Royal Yachting Association (registered in
the United Kingdom and selected marketing territories).

† Coastal Skipper and Day Skipper are unregistered
trademarks of the Royal Yachting Association.

**For a free, full-colour brochure write,
phone, fax or email us:**

Fernhurst Books, Duke's Path, High
Street, Arundel, West Sussex, BN18 9AJ,
United Kingdom.
Phone: 01903 882277
Fax: 01903 882715
Email: sales@fernhurstbooks.co.uk
Website: www.fernhurstbooks.co.uk

Contents

Welcome to Navigation

Navigation is something we all do: it is simply finding the way around.

We negotiate the motorways and rail systems using maps and signs. We have learnt to read the maps, follow the signs, look out for landmarks and study timetables. We estimate how long the journey will take allowing for the distance and the average speed that we expect to travel, and then add on a bit because of possible delays. If it is somewhere we have not been before we read up about it and talk to friends for advice. This is navigation.

The aim of this book is to help transfer these skills of navigation from the land to the sea.

Someone once said to me that there are only two questions in navigation:
Where am I? ....
(see pages 22-37 Finding your position)
Where do I go now?.........
(see pages 51-65 Course to steer)
While I agree with this generally, there are other background details that need to be included to help answer the two basic questions.

To help make the book easy to use the different subjects are colour-coded and the details are built up gradually.

Navigation is fun and remember – it can't be that difficult because lots of people can do it! **Sara.**

Some of the vast range of electronic navigation equipment available.

Looking at charts: 1
Types of chart

The place to start if you are interested in navigation at sea is with **charts**, which are the maps of the sea. These are full of fascinating details, not of the land or of the sea really, but of the coast and what lies beneath the water. Data has been gathered over many centuries by navigators and explorers and now satellite technology is used to enhance the accuracy. Look on a chart for the **source data** to see the date of the surveys used to produce it.

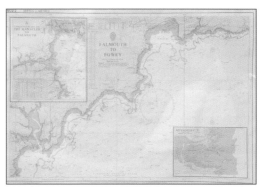

A standard format chart.

Source data.

Charts concentrate on the details that are of interest to navigators such as:

* The depth of the water.
* Hazards, like rocks and sandbanks.
* Conspicuous features on the coastline.
* Points of navigational importance like lighthouses and buoys.

Many details on the land are omitted as not relevant.

The best chart to start studying is one of an area that you have sailed in or know from the land.

Ordinary bookshops that sell maps do not generally sell charts and most marina chandlers only stock a few charts of the local area, so for the best selection and advice search out a **chart agent**. Chart agents specialise in selling charts. They stock charts and navigation publications for the world.

There are different makes of charts.

Admiralty charts. These are the charts produced by an agency of the government, the UK Hydrographic Office. They produce charts and books for use throughout the world. The **standard format chart** is large, approximately 1m x 0.75 m, which can be inconvenient to use or to store with a small chart table, or no chart table at all. These charts can only be bought from Admiralty chart agents and are quite expensive. This cost is to allow for the chart being totally correct at the time that it is purchased. All charts become out-of-date quite quickly as depths change or buoys are moved, but a chart agent will hand-correct a chart every week if necessary. After you have bought the chart, it is down to you to keep it up to date. Information can be found in booklets called Notices to Mariners bought from chart agents, downloaded from the Admiralty website on **www.nmwebsearch.com** or in some boating magazines.

Additionally the HO (Hydro-graphic Office) produces a **leisure series** of charts. These are identical in chart detail but are on thinner paper, have information printed on the reverse side and are sold folded to about **A4 size**. It is important to know that these charts are **not** corrected once they have been printed, that is why they are cheaper and can be bought through chandlers. Leisure charts can also be bought in **folios** of about 10 charts in A2 format covering the most popular leisure boating areas. These are

Folio of leisure charts.

very good value and come in a strong plastic wallet, but you have no choice of chart or of scale.

From 2004 the leisure folios have been available as the **Admiralty RYA* Electronic**

Chart Plotter. These electronic charts work on a computer and each disc is licensed for a year. To renew or update you must buy a new disc. These charts look the same as the paper version but the plotter can do navigation calculations in addition to displaying the charts. For more information on any of the UKHO products go to **www.ukho.gov.uk**

Imray Charts are produced by Imray, Laurie, Norie and Wilson. They are sold through chart agents and chandlers and cover the UK, Mediterranean and Caribbean. Their charts come singly or in folios and are on waterproof paper. Imray produce many pilot books of popular areas specially written for skippers of yachts and motor cruisers, whereas the Admiralty publications were originally intended for ship captains.

* Denotes a trademark registered by the RYA.

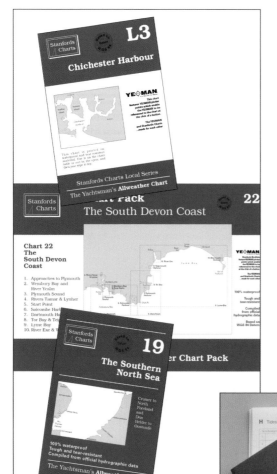

Foreign charts are quite similar in appearance and worth considering. The Dutch charts of their inland waterways, for example, are full of detail and so popular that they can be bought in chandlers in the UK.

Many of the symbols used on charts are easy to guess but others have to be learnt……it's best to do this a few at a time as there are hundreds! The UKHO publishes a fantastic book: **Symbols and Abbreviations used on Admiralty Charts**. This is often called **5011** by old hands, as this is the old chart number dating from the time when the information was produced as a chart. This is a useful addition to every boat's library. The information is published for Admiralty charts, but the symbols are largely common to all chart producers.

Many of the **chart symbols** are easy to guess because they are simply very small pictures of the real object. Each picture obviously

Stanfords Charts cover areas of the UK and near continent and come on folded sheets or in folios. All are on waterproof and tearproof paper. Again these are produced with the needs of owners of small boats, not ships, in mind.

Electronic charts are becoming increasingly popular and are used with a computer, like the Admiralty RYA* series, or with a dedicated plotter with an electronic display. As well as the Admiralty, private companies produce these charts. More about these later, but remember these need updating too.

takes up much more space on the paper than the real thing so a small circle in the baseline shows the actual position.　—○—

Many people starting their first navigation course immediately consider a new pair of glasses!

Here are a few of the common and
important symbols:

  A north cardinal buoy, unlit.

BY

 Red buoy, with light.

R

 Rock awash at the level of
chart datum.

 Green buoy, unlit.

G

 Underwater rock over which
the exact depth is unknown
but which is considered
dangerous to surface
navigation.

 Wreck, depth unknown, not
considered dangerous to
surface navigation.

 Remains of a wreck,
or other obstruction,
no longer dangerous to
surface navigation, but to be
avoided by vessels anchoring,
trawling etc.

 Wreck, depth unknown, but
considered dangerous to
surface navigation.

 Wk Wreck over which the depth
has been obtained by
sounding not by wire sweep.

 Obstruction.

Obstn

 Wk Wreck which has been swept
by wire to the depth shown.

 Wk Wreck over which the exact
depth is unknown but which is
considered to have a safe
clearance to the depth shown.

 Major light or lighthouse.

 Wreck showing part of hull or
superstructure at the level of
chart datum.

 Beacon, with light.

BY

 Prohibited area.

 Rock which covers and
uncovers, showing height
above chart datum where
known.

Overfalls.

Looking at Charts: 2
Depths and heights

A non-metric chart.

A metric chart.

Most charts, but not all, are now **metric** and instantly recognisable because they are so colourful... and say 'DEPTHS IN METRES' on the white margins at the top and bottom of the chart! This means that the depths of water and the heights of bridges and lighthouses are given in metres. On **non-metric charts** the depths are in feet and fathoms (6 feet equals 1 fathom) and the heights in feet. On comparison the non-metric charts seem quite dull because the colours are mainly limited to black and white.

On Admiralty metric charts one of the main uses of colour is to make the different depths stand out vividly:

- **Yellow** is used to show the area above sea level... land!
- **Green** shows areas like beaches, rocks, mudflats and sandbanks which are sometimes covered by the water and sometimes not. These are known as drying areas.

- **Dark blue**, **light blue** and then **white** show increasing depth of water.

These areas are separated by **marine contour lines**. Follow a contour line and somewhere along it will be written the number of metres that it represents.

Don't expect to find the shallow areas only along the coastline. The sandbanks of the Thames Estuary are famous, or infamous! The banks fan out to form a complicated maze of channels as the River Thames flows out into the North Sea. It is possible for a boat to be aground in the Thames Estuary but unable to see land at all, and in bad weather boats have been smashed to pieces on these dangerous banks. Similarly the Bramble Bank in the Solent has caught out many sailors who go aground close to the main shipping channel to Southampton Docks.

All these banks are clearly marked on the chart but skippers need to navigate with care and remember the old saying "The nearest bit of land to you is usually the bit underneath the boat!"

Depth of water may be one of the most vital bits of information for navigators but it is not straightforward to show on a chart because the depth varies as the water goes up and down with the tide.

This problem is solved by relating the depths to **chart datum** as a theoretical level from which to start measuring.

Chart datum is usually defined as the **lowest astronomical tide**. Astronomical since it is the positions of the sun and the moon that cause the movement of the water that we call tides. The level shown on the chart is therefore pessimistic, as it shows the lowest level to which the water is expected to fall, except under extreme weather conditions or abnormal range of the tide. (The **range of the tide** is the amount the water has gone up or down between high water and low water.)

Range = HW - LW

In other words there is almost always some more water than is shown on the chart - at high water there is a lot more and at low water there is a little more. Showing the least depth ever expected increases the safety margin. The numbers written over the blue and white areas of the chart are the **charted depths** in meters, known as **soundings**. They are written without the use of a decimal point but show the figure for the decimal below the main number.

$1_7 = 1.7\text{m}$ $24_6 = 24.6\text{m}$

If it is necessary to know the actual **depth of water** at a particular spot then the **height of tide** would have to be added

to the charted depth shown on the chart. (The height of tide is how much the water is above chart datum. For high water and low water height of tide can be found in tide tables. Height of tide between high water and low water can be calculated if necessary. See Figure 1.)

Height of tide + charted depth = depth of water

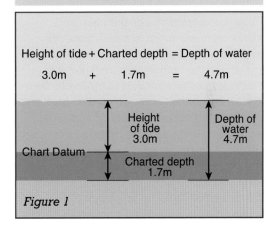

Height of tide + Charted depth = Depth of water
3.0m   +   1.7m   =   4.7m

Chart Datum

Height of tide 3.0m

Charted depth 1.7m

Depth of water 4.7m

Figure 1

Another feature associated with depth shown by colour and figures is **drying height**. This is an area **above chart datum**, which therefore may 'dry out' or stick out above the water most of the time, some of the time or just occasionally. Drying heights are shown in **green with the figures underlined** showing the height in metres above chart datum (Figure 2).

$\underline{0}_5 = \text{dries } 0.5\text{m}$ $\underline{1}_8 = \text{dries } 1.8\text{m}$

above chart datum

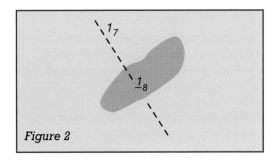

Figure 2

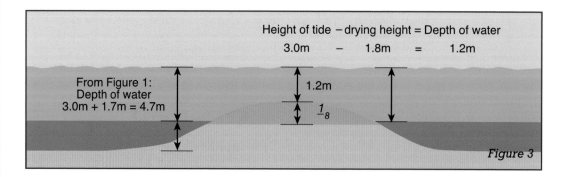

Height of tide − drying height = Depth of water

3.0m   −   1.8m   =   1.2m

From Figure 1:
Depth of water
3.0m + 1.7m = 4.7m

1.2m

1_8

Figure 3

These areas are found on the coast and where there are rocks or sandbanks, but again the height of the tide must be taken into account to calculate the real danger. **The height of tide must be applied to the drying height** that is shown on the chart, and may cancel it out completely. The chart is being pessimistic again to increase the safety margin. Remember there is almost always more water than is shown on the chart.

This is a good thing up to a point. The green areas are not always above the level of the water, even though they are above the level of chart datum. Skippers can see them on the chart but not always by eye - if they could maybe fewer people would hit them! Sometimes there is no water over a sandbank at all and the seals may be sunning themselves, sometimes there is enough water to sail right over the bank quite safely and sometimes there is water over the bank so that it cannot be seen ...but not enough! All this depends on the height of the tide (Figure 3).

Height of tide – drying height = depth of water

The colours and figures help the navigator to build up the 'three dimensional' image necessary to navigate in rivers, estuaries and coastal areas (Figure 3).

Is all information about heights given with reference to chart datum?

Well no, it is not. The exceptions are **the height of a lighthouse or the elevation of a bridge**. These are given with reference to **MHWS** (Mean High Water Springs) (Figure 4). MHWS is the height of the tide at the average, or mean, of the highest high tides, which are called spring tides. Spring tides occur all the year round, not just in spring! More about this later.

Usually the height of the tide is lower than MHWS (Figure 5), so the lighthouse is in

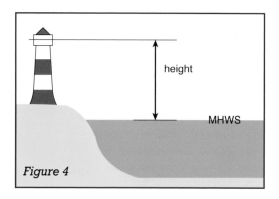

height

MHWS

Figure 4

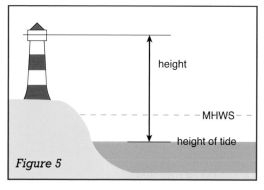

height

MHWS

height of tide

Figure 5

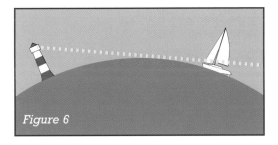

Figure 6

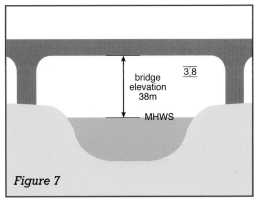

Figure 7

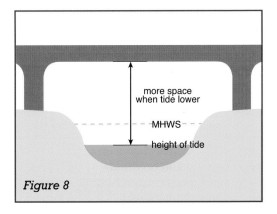

Figure 8

effect 'taller' than shown on the chart and so can be seen further away (Figure 6). With a bridge or power cable a captain calculating whether the ship can pass underneath can be sure that the elevation shown on the chart will be the minimum. When the height of tide is lower than MHWS there will be more clearance than shown (Figures 7 & 8).

The information given on the chart is again pessimistic, to increase the safety margin.

When taking a good look at a chart don't miss the information shown in the notices. Somewhere on the chart is a panel of information about the chart itself and special details and warnings for the local area. This information will include:

• **The datum of the chart**. This the measuring system that was used to produce the chart. Our charts used to be marked OSGB 36 for Ordnance Survey of Great Britain 1936 but UK charts are now all WGS84 meaning that they are based on the World Geodetic Survey of 1984.
Do you need to know this? Yes, to some extent. If a satellite navigation system, such as GPS, in used on the boat it will need to be set to the same datum as the chart to prevent inaccuracies. It is necessary to go into the main menu system to do this, and maybe read the instruction book too!

• **The buoyage system for the region.**

There are only two systems, Region A and Region B. North America, and other countries nearby, use Region B but everywhere else uses Region A. This will be dealt with later in the book. It's not as confusing as it seems but check up before that exotic charter or diving holiday!

• **Projection**. This is the method that was used to make the round world fit on a flat piece of paper. This has been a problem ever since the first charts were drawn and different solutions or projections are still used. All result in some distortions of scale.

• **Local safety notes and warnings.** It's a good idea to read these: if they were not important they would not have been put on the chart in the first place!

Giving a position: 1
Latitude and longitude

Having looked at a chart and understood some of the symbols and colours the next thing to tackle is **position**. The position is a description of an **exact location** on the surface of the planet. I am going to cover this is two parts:

• How to describe to another navigator where you are.
• How to find out where you are......
  that's in the next section.

The most well-known method of describing a position that can be plotted on a chart is by using **latitude and longitude**. These lines run round the world horizontally and from pole to pole to form a grid.

When latitude and longitude are used to name a position, **latitude is always given first**.

The grid is made up of **parallels of latitude** running north and south of the equator. The lines are not the same length, as they become shorter towards the poles, but

they are parallel. The line 52⁰ could be 52⁰ N, close to Ipswich in Suffolk or 52⁰ S running south of Australia, so latitude must be marked N or S to make sense. The 52⁰ is the angle from the centre of the earth (see Figure 9.).

Superimposed upon these lines are the **meridians of longitude** measured east and west from Greenwich. These lines are all the same length, but obviously not parallel. The line 1⁰ E runs close to Ipswich and should be written as 001⁰ E to make it clearly different from 010⁰ E or 100⁰ E (see Figure 10). It's a bit like writing a cheque, where you put the zeros makes a lot of difference! Marking the longitude E or W is vital too. The 001⁰ is the angle between that line of longitude and the **prime meridian** or 000⁰, which runs through The Royal Observatory at Greenwich, in London.

The position of 52⁰ N 001⁰ E for Ipswich is approximately correct but imprecise. For added detail **each degree is divided into 60 minutes, and each minute into tenths**. Using this format the position for Ipswich

Figure 9

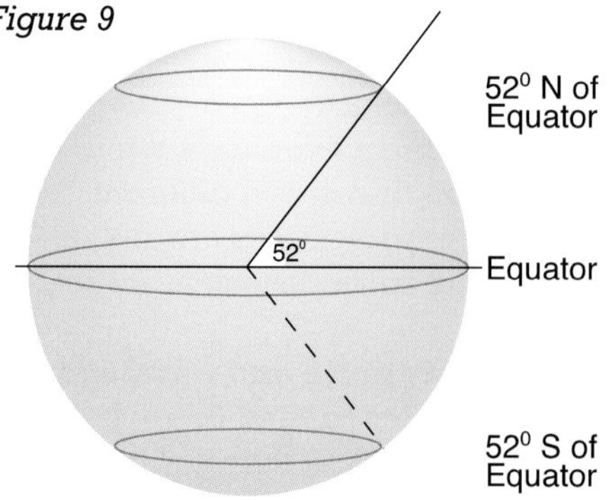

52⁰ N of Equator

52⁰

Equator

52⁰ S of Equator

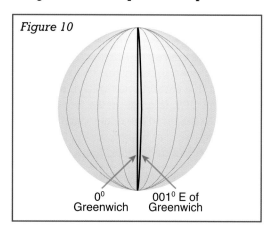

Figure 10

0⁰
Greenwich

001⁰ E of Greenwich

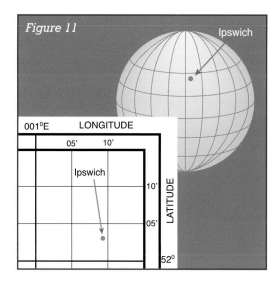

Figure 11

001°E LONGITUDE

Ipswich

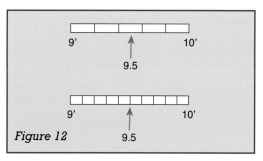

9'   10'

9.5

9'   10'

Figure 12   9.5

Each minute is divided up depending on the scale of the chart, and the only way to know the value of each small subdivision is by counting (Figure 12).

How to measure latitude and longitude from the chart

becomes: 52° 03'.5 N 001° 09'.5 E (see Figure 11) . The placing of the each zero, minute symbol and decimal point is vital to make the meaning correct, as is the use of the N and E.

When this simple grid system is moved from the round world to a flat piece of paper:

*   The latitude scale is found at either side of the chart.
*   The longitude scale is at the top and the bottom.

An easy way of measuring the latitude and longitude is with the use of dividers. These are traditionally made of brass and shaped for single-handed use, so the navigator can hold on in a rough sea. Hopefully that won't be necessary too often!

Measure the distance relative to a line of latitude and then transfer that to the scale at either side of the chart. Count carefully because the appearance of the scale will differ from chart to chart.

Dividers

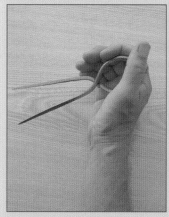

1. *Hold the dividers like this.*

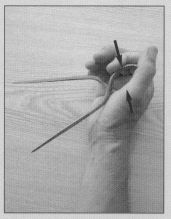

2. *Squeeze the curved parts to open the dividers.*

3. *Push the straight parts to close them.*

Finding the latitude and longitude of a point on a chart

1. *Use the dividers to measure from the object to the nearest line of latitude, in this case the 50⁰ 15' line.*

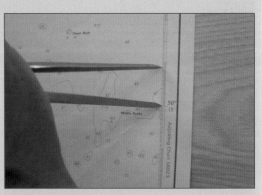

2. *Move the dividers to the latitude scale and read off the exact latitude, 50⁰ 15'.9 N.*

3. *Now measure from the object to the nearest line of longitude, in this case the 004⁰ 40' line.*

4. *Now move the dividers to the longitude scale and read off the exact longitude, 004⁰ 39'.1 W.*

Repeat the exercise to measure the longitude, using the scale at the top or bottom of the chart, and remember that latitude is always given first (see panel above).

How to measure distances from the chart

Dividers are also used for measuring distances across the chart from place to place. On the chart the **distances** are measured using the **latitude scale** never, never the longitude scale. Although the appearance of each degree and minute of latitude will differ depending on whether the chart is covering a large or small area one fact is always true.

**1 minute of latitude = 1 nautical mile
1' of latitude = 1 mile**

So to measure the distance one point of the dividers is placed on each object and then that measurement is moved to the latitude scale to count the distance carefully (see panel opposite).

This simple scale is not perfect because of the distortions between the round world and a flat chart. Chart makers have made adjustments to allow for this by using different projections, so on a chart covering a very large area it is possible to measure a mile at the north

How to measure distances from a chart

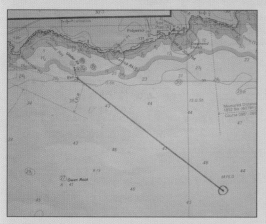

1. *Measuring a distance from the chart, in this case from the buoy to the circle (fix).*

2. *Open the dividers the required distance.*

of the chart and a mile at the south of the chart and find them different! This seems a bit surreal but is not so bad in practice. **Always use the part of the latitude scale that is nearest** to where you are plotting. This will avoid the problem, and it is convenient as well.

To measure a distance quickly and approximately open the dividers to a convenient number, perhaps 5 or 10 miles, and then 'walk' them across the chart counting as the dividers are turned (Figure 13).

3. *Transfer to the nearby* latitude *scale and read off the distance (1' = 1M). In this case it is 4 miles.*

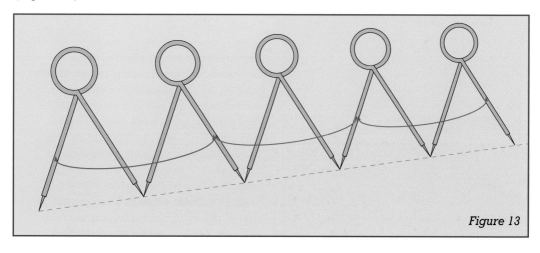

Figure 13

Giving a position: 2
Range and bearing

Latitude and longitude are not the only way to tell someone your position, and in fact it may not even be the best way. It can be very accurate and easy to measure, especially if the boat has an electronic navigation system, like GPS, but it is not very 'user friendly' for the recipient of the information.

For example, if I told people that I lived approximately 52⁰ 03'.5 N 001⁰ 09'.5 E not many would have any idea where that was. On the other hand if I said "I live north east of London, about 70 miles" they can imagine that immediately. To a local I can use a well-known landmark. I usually say "I live down the lane to the pub, about a quarter of a mile".

This method of giving a position is used at sea as well and is called a **range and bearing**. It is very easy for the person hearing the information to understand or to plot on the chart. They start at the well-known place and draw or imagine a line in that direction for the distance mentioned.

(Despite being called a range and bearing, the direction or **bearing <u>from</u> the named place is always given first**.)

To give the **direction** in navigation we no longer use the traditional 32 point compass with directions like 'north by north-north-west' but the 360 degrees of a circle instead. This is shown on the chart for reference on the compass rose. On most charts there are several compass roses.

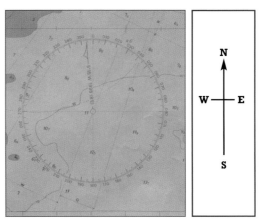

A compass rose.

It is important to get a feel of these directions to make drawing and measuring lines on the chart easier. For example north is referred to as 000⁰ and south as 180⁰. Three digits are always used so east becomes 090⁰, and the 0 is said as "zero". Remember when drawing a line along a ruler it can go in either direction, up as well as down. The easiest mistake to make is to draw a line as a reciprocal, so always check against the compass rose until you have a feel for the directions.

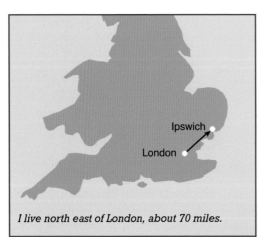

I live north east of London, about 70 miles.

Putting these together the position of a boat two miles south of the Sunk Light-vessel off Harwich becomes '180⁰ from Sunk Light Vessel 2 miles'.

To measure the direction from the chart various plotting instruments or rulers are available.

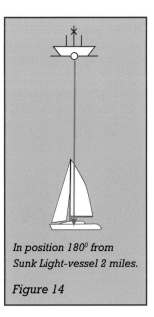

In position 180⁰ from Sunk Light-vessel 2 miles.

Figure 14

Traditionally **a parallel ruler** was used on ships.

To use a parallel ruler place either the top or bottom edge along the direction to be measured and then carefully transfer it to the nearest compass roseby 'walking' the ruler across the chart (see panel below). When one edge is lined up through the centre of the compass rose read the answer from the outer ring. If the ruler slips then start again.

It only takes practice to use a parallel ruler quickly, but they can be very awkward on a small chart table where there is not really room to walk them across the chart.

Using a parallel ruler to measure the bearing of AB

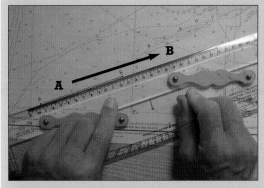

1. *Lay the rule along the line.*

2. *'Walk' the rule towards the compass rose.*

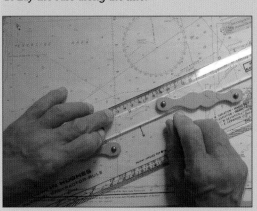

3.

4. *Read off the angle, in this case 070⁰.*

The best plotting aid that I have found and the one that I would recommend is the **'Breton' type plotter**. A Breton type plotter has a movable protractor disc so there is no need to slide it across the chart to the compass rose. This is much more convenient on a small chart table.

How to use the plotter

The plotter can be used in two ways

* To measure the direction from one position to another on the chart.
* To draw a line on the chart in a chosen direction.

How to measure directions from a chart

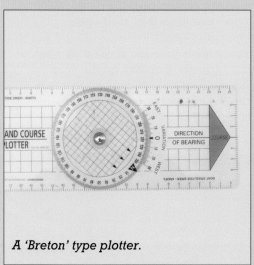

A 'Breton' type plotter.

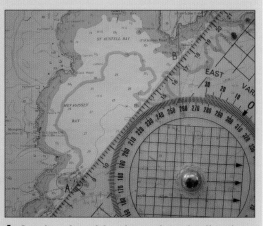

1. *Lay the edge of the plotter along the direction to be measured (A-B).*

Take care to point the large coloured arrow on the plotter in the direction that you want to measure.

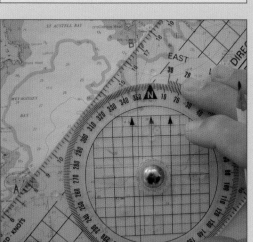

2. *Turn the protractor disc so that N is pointing north and the grid on the disc is lined up with a line of latitude or longitude on the chart beneath.*

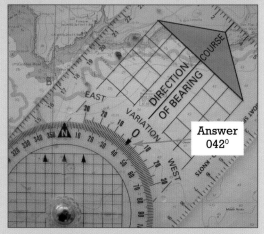

Answer 042⁰

3. *Read off the answer where the central line of the plotter meets the protractor (in this case 042 ⁰). Check the answer by estimating, using the compass rose. Ask yourself "Does that seem about right?" Always test measurements and calculations against this common sense rule.*

How to draw a line on a chart

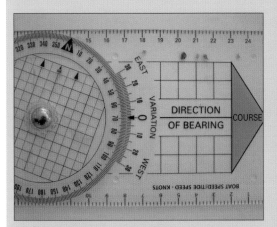

1. *Turn the protractor disc so the direction to be drawn is lined up with the central line of the plotter (e.g. 070 [0]).*

2. *Place a pencil on the position on the chart that you are drawing from and put the plotter against it.*

3. *Align the plotter so that the N is pointing north by sliding and rotating the plotter (using the pencil as a pivot) until the grid on the protractor is lined up with a line of latitude or longitude on the chart beneath.*

4. *Draw the line in the direction of the large cloloured arrow on the plotter.*
Check the line by estimating against the compass rose. Remember the easiest mistake to make is to draw a line as a reciprocal (that is, in exactly the opposite direction).

Finding your position: 1 GPS

Real navigation at last, **finding a position**, and the first chart plotting symbol used by navigators.

A position plotted by a navigator is marked with a circle and the time.

Keeping a sense of the boat's position is vital in the three-dimensional world of the sea. Unfortunately it is not as straightforward as on land. The sea has few features to recognise and no one to ask if you get lost, and other problems too. Luckily there are instruments to help. As the boat travels forward the ships **steering compass** will show the direction that the boat is heading and the **log** will measure the distance travelled, but there are unseen forces acting on the boat.

- The **wind** may push the boat sideways causing **leeway**. This affects different-shaped boats to a greater or lesser extent, increases with the force of the wind and varies with the wind direction relative to the boats heading. Leeway is difficult to measure and has to be estimated from the conditions at the time and the type of boat.

- The whole body of water may be moving too because of a **tidal stream**. This is the **horizontal movement** of the water caused by the ebb and flow of the tides. All vessels and other free-floating objects are affected to the same extent because it is the water that is moving. Tidal streams may increase or decrease the speed of the boat or push the vessel off the heading that the helmsman is steering. This does **not** show on the log and has to be calculated.

So checking the position regularly and **keeping a record in the logbook** is important.

There are lots of ways of checking the position, some quicker than others, some more reliable than others and it is best to use a variety of methods to avoid putting all your nautical eggs in one basket. Never just assume that a position is correct. Look for corroborating evidence and apply the common sense test:

- Does this make sense with what I can see and with the last known position?

Don't assume you are wrong either, in fact don't assume anything! Remember as well that by the time you have plotted the position on the chart you are not there any more! Even if the boat is travelling at only 6 knots, in 10 minutes it will have travelled a mile.

One of the biggest changes in navigation in recent years has been the introduction of electronic position fixing devices with ever-increasing accuracy. First Decca and Loran and now GPS have transformed the work of the navigator. GPS can find the position and then update it automatically every few seconds.

GPS (Global Position System)
A GPS receiver uses information from several satellites to calculate its position. They are remarkably accurate, inexpensive and work world-wide.

The set needs an antenna that can 'see the sky', so many handheld sets will not work down below on the boat. With a fixed set the aerial should be mounted low down to give the best results and remember to set the datum for the chart that you are using.

Most sets show the position as a latitude and longitude, sometimes to three places of decimals, which is perhaps a little misleading. The average calculated accuracy of a GPS set is within 5 metres 95% of the time. Some sets display the position on a chart image on a chart plotter or computer or the position can be fed into other equipment on the boat such as a VHF/DSC radio or a radar set.

Once the set knows the position it can then compute other very useful information, but to get the best of all these other extra features you will have to read the instruction book! Remember that whatever other information the set displays, **GPS is essentially a position-fixing device** and it knows nothing about depth of water or tidal streams. In fact most boats that go aground on sandbanks or hit rocks probably have GPS!

The GPS can display the position in different ways, such as:

- Latitude and longitude.
- Reference to a waypoint.

These will not give a different position. They cannot be used first one and then the other to check if the position is correct. It is the same information presented in a different way. GPS cannot check itself: new data from another source would need to be introduced to make a worthwhile check of a position.

The choice of display is personal to the skipper and for ease of plotting onto the chart. Using the position displayed with reference to a waypoint can make plotting much quicker and easier than using latitude and longitude.

Plotting the position from the latitude and longitude display

From the GPS the latitude and longitude information can be plotted onto the chart using dividers or plotter.

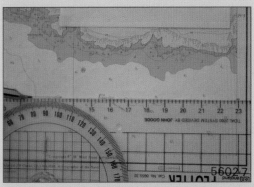

1. *Start with the latitude and line the plotter up on the latitude scale, taking care to count the decimal places accurately.*
Make sure that the plotter is horizontal using the lines of latitude.
Draw a short line at approximately the right longitude.

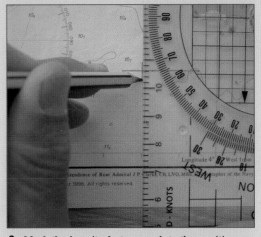

2. *Mark the longitude to complete the position.*

If the plotter is not long enough to line up and keep the lines level and perpendicular, use the dividers for both latitude and longitude.

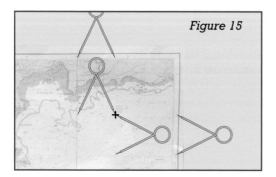

Figure 15

On a small chart table when the chart has to be folded the latitude and longitude scales may be inaccessible so plotting the position with reference to a waypoint can be easier.

What exactly is a waypoint?

A waypoint is any navigation mark or point on the chart chosen by the navigator. The latitude and longitude of the waypoint are programmed into the GPS. The set will then display the **direction and distance to the waypoint**, updating as the boat moves.

The original idea behind this feature on a GPS set was that waypoints along a route could be selected and displayed during the passage. The directions shown could not be followed blindly, of course, because the GPS has no information about the wind and the tidal streams. Nevertheless, the route feature can be extremely useful, although accidents have occurred when:

- An unsafe waypoint has been chosen, crossing shallow water or rocks.

- **The latitude and longitude of the waypoint has been put into the GPS incorrectly.**
- Boats have hit a buoy used as a waypoint.
- Many skippers have chosen the same waypoint.
- Skippers have not recorded information into the logbook and then suffered a failure of the set.
- Skippers have not checked their position, just followed the machine blindly.
- The GPS has not been set to the same datum as the chart.
- Navigators have not allowed for tidal streams and leeway.

GPS is really great, but use with care.

A waypoint is marked on the chart with a cross and a box.

Plotting a position with reference to a waypoint

You can use a waypoint to make plotting positions quicker and easier than latitude and longitude (see the panel on page 26). The waypoint does not have to be a place on the route, or a buoy or anything real at all. It can be any point that is convenient and easy to see:

- The centre of the compass rose is simple for plotting because the compass is there (see the panel on page 25).
- A cross of latitude and longitude lines is quick to programme into the GPS.
- A buoy or convenient mark.

Remember the GPS will always show **direction and distance *to* the waypoint**, because *it thinks that you want to go there!*

Plotting using the compass rose as a waypoint

1. *In this case the direction to the waypoint is **240°** and the distance is **3.60** miles. The waypoint is the centre of the compass rose.*

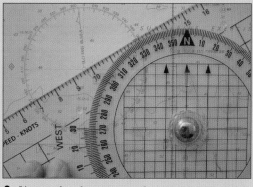

2. *Line up the plotter across the compass rose using the centre spot and 240° on the far side of the rose.*

3. *Draw a short line in the direction towards the centre of the rose.*

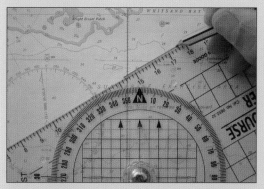

4. *Set the dividers to the distance shown, here 3.60 miles.*

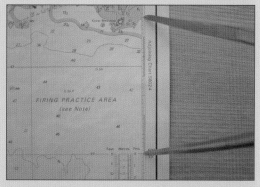

5. *Measure this distance.*

6. *Mark the position. Then add a circle and the time, with an arrow pointing towards the waypoint.*

time

Plotting a postion from a waypoint

1. In this case the direction to the waypoint is **030** ⁰ and the distance is **2.40** miles. The waypoint has been chosen by the navigator.

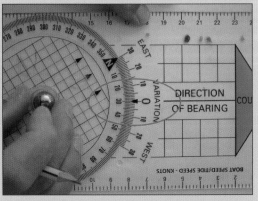

2. On the plotter set the direction towards the waypoint by turning the protractor disc, here 030 ⁰.

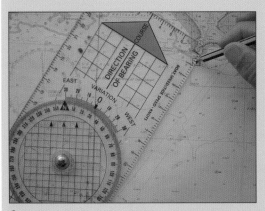

3. Put the pencil on the waypoint and the plotter against it. Slide and rotate the plotter (using the pencil as a pivot) until the grid on the protractor is lined up with the lines of latitude and longitude on the chart beneath, and the N is pointing north.

4. Draw a short line.

5. Measure the distance to the waypoint, here 2.4 miles.

6. Mark the position. Then add a circle and the time, with an arrow pointing towards the waypoint.

time

Finding your position: 2
A fix

Navigators often spend a great deal of time at the chart table, perhaps trying to calculate the boat's position, and sometimes miss easy opportunities to check the position visually. This is especially true in coastal navigation.

Finding or fixing a position, without the use of GPS, can be done by **observation**.

- If the boat is passing close to a buoy then this will give a **fix of position** (well almost a fix, as buoys do drift a little on their anchor chains).
- If a buoy or better still an object on the land can be seen clearly enough to be identified then a **bearing** can be taken with a hand-bearing compass. Plotted on the chart this bearing gives a position line, because we know that the boat is somewhere on that line. One **position line** will not give a fix of position, of course. Two bearings will give a cross, because the two lines are bound to cross somewhere, unless they are parallel or diverging, so three bearings are needed to give a **fix of position**. This is known as a three-point fix.

- If two objects that can be identified clearly and are marked on the chart are seen to **come into line** this will form a **transit** that can be drawn on the chart as a position line without the need to take a bearing. Again, one position line is not enough, but it can be combined with a bearing to give a **fix of position**. Just two lines is OK this time because the transit is so accurate.

Taking a fix of position using three bearings ...a three-point-fix

1 Check on the chart and look around for suitable objects to use to take the bearings:
- Objects that you can see and identify clearly.
- Objects more than 30^0 apart so the lines cross at a good angle.
- Objects not 180^0 apart, or the lines will be parallel and not cross at all.
- Objects not too far away because the longer the line the greater the inaccuracy.
- Objects on land are the most reliable as their position never moves.
2 Take the three bearings as quickly as

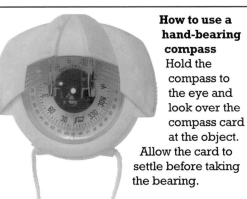

How to use a hand-bearing compass
Hold the compass to the eye and look over the compass card at the object. Allow the card to settle before taking the bearing.

possible, but allow time for the compass card to settle.

3 Take the bearing on the beam (the side of the boat) last, as it is changing most rapidly.

4 When the bearings have been written down note the **reading from the log** that shows how far the boat has moved and the **time**. It can sometimes be useful to note the depth reading on the echosounder too.

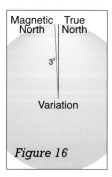

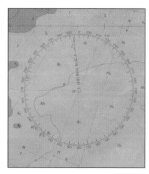

Figure 16

But....

Unfortunately, before these bearings can be plotted on the chart there is one small problem that must be dealt with.

Compass variation

Variation is caused by the way that the compass works. Most on small boats are magnetic compasses and show north by sensing the earth's magnetic field. Thus they point to **magnetic** north and not to **true** north, which unfortunately are not at the same place. True north is at the top of the world (where the stick comes out of a globe, where all the lines of longitude meet) but magnetic north is in northern Canada.

Variation:
- **Is the angular difference between true and magnetic north expressed in degrees.**
- Varies from place to place in the world.
- Can be E or W depending on the location.
- Affects both steering compasses and hand-bearing compasses.
- Affects all compasses in an area the same, so there is no point in buying a new one!
- Changes very, very slowly with time.
- Is shown on the compass rose.

On a compass rose it might say 3^0 10' **W**. 2000. (7' **E**). This means that when the chart was printed the variation was 3^0 10' **W**. This would be rounded to 3^0W, the nearest degree, in all calculations (Figure 16). The (7' E) means that the variation is changing by 7 minutes every

year. It takes 60' to make 1^0 so it will take over eight years for the variation to change by a whole degree. From one side of the chart to the other the variation may well be different by a few minutes.

To calculate the exact variation in this position:
- Multiply 7' x the number of years since 2000, add or subtract this figure from the 2000 variation. Then round to the nearest whole degree.

For 2005 that is 7' x 5 = 35' **E**.
3^0 10' W - 35' **E** = 2^0 35' W, rounded to 3^0 **W**

In this example the change of 7' was E and **different** from the W variation of the chart, therefore it was **subtracted**. If the designation is the **same** then **add**.

Always correct for the variation to any compass reading <u>before</u> plotting it on a chart, because charts are printed based on true north.

Add or subtract the variation to the compass reading depending on whether the variation in the area is E or W.

To convert a **magnetic** reading from a compass to **true** to plot on the chart

- **subtract a westerly variation**
- **add an easterly variation**

Friends will tell you rhymes to help you

remember whether to add or subtract, which may or may not help. If necessary write it on the top and bottom of the chart, write it on the plotter, or stick it up by the chart table. Most important is to become familiar with how to apply variation in your local area. All variation in the UK is **west** for example, ranging from 6° W in the Irish Sea to 3° W in the North Sea.

My favourite mnemonic is

   C A D E T for Compass to True add E…
   +E so -W

If the variation is W do the opposite

How to plot a three-point fix:
- Convert the magnetic bearings to true.
- On the plotter set the protractor to the true bearing.

- Place a pencil on the object from which the bearing was taken with the arrow on the plotter pointing towards it and the N pointing north.
- Slide and rotate the plotter (using the pencil as a pivot) to line up the grid of the protractor with the latitude and longitude lines on the chart beneath.
- Draw in the bearing in approximately the right place. It is better not to draw the full length of the line to avoid clutter on the chart.
- Plot the other bearings.
- Mark each bearing with an arrowhead pointing away from the object. Mark the fix with a circle.
- Write the time beside the fix. The time of the fix is **when the bearings were taken**, because that is when you were there, not the time that the plot is finished.

Plotting a three point fix

1. Plot the bearing of the headland.

2. Next, plot the bearing of the western end of the breakwater.

3. Finally, plot the bearing of the last object.

4. The resulting 'cocked hat'.

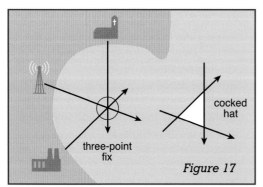

Figure 17

Don't expect it to be perfect. Usually there is a small triangle called a 'cocked hat'. This is because the boat was moving forwards while the bearings were taken, and maybe up and down as well! If the cocked hat is huge then check the working. Forgetting to convert from magnetic to true will produce quite a large triangle.

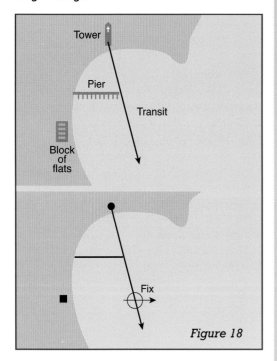

Figure 18

Plotting a transit

Two objects that are seen to line up give a transit that can be plotted on the chart. No maths, just draw what you can see. One bearing, corrected for variation, gives a fix (Figure 18). Quick and accurate.

Transit bearing fix

1. *The breakwater and a buoy form a transit.*

2. *Add the bearing of the headland...*

3. *...to give a fix. Finally mark each line with an arrow.*

Finding your position: 3
A DR position

Away from land, especially without GPS, fixing the position can be much more difficult and navigators have to deduce their position using the instruments and written records, such as:

- A steering compass to measure the **direction** the boat is heading.
- A log to measure the **distance** travelled.
- A logbook to record this information at regular intervals.

In the early days the measurements were crude but modern instruments still need checking for accuracy. A **compass** may read inaccurately because of magnetic influences on the boat causing compass **deviation**. Wiring, mobile phones, loudspeakers, batteries, hand-held flares, the engine or even the keel can cause the compass to read inaccurately if they are too close. A **log** may under-read, or even stop, if the impeller is fouled by weed. Under-reading is especially dangerous as the boat may hit the hazard long before it was expected to be close. The instrument will often have a duel display showing the speed that the boat is travelling through the water and the total distance. Usually there is a 'trip' as well so that the distance can be set to zero at the beginning of each passage for easier maths.

Plotting the **direction** sailed and **distance** travelled will give an approximate position known as a **DR position**. DR is an abbreviation for 'Dead Reckoning', which does not seem to make much sense as a name until you know it was an abbreviation from the original expression 'Deduced Reckoning'.

A basic DR is simple to use and quick to plot, but does not give a fix of position with anything like the accuracy of GPS or a three-point fix because it ignores:

- Tidal streams which may be pushing the boat forwards, backwards or sideways.
- Leeway (wind effect) which may be pushing the boat sideways.

But it is better than nothing, and can be improved by allowing for tidal streams and leeway or by fixing the position by another method when it becomes possible.

Keeping a logbook

This is a vitally important record of the navigational details of the passage. The direction steered, alterations of course, log readings and GPS positions **must** all be written down. Many skippers also choose to record details of the wind strength and direction, depth shown on the echosounder, barometer readings, engine readings and even events like change of watches, change of sails or the sighting of dolphins. A ruled out notebook can be used but printed logbooks suitable for different kinds of boats are also available. They have the advantage of prompting the navigator to include all the important and useful details.

How to plot a DR position

- Convert the **magnetic** heading that the helmsman has been steering to **true**.
- Set the true heading on the plotter.
- Place the pencil on the last position, and put the plotter against it.
- Slide and rotate the plotter, using the pencil as a pivot, until it is lined up with the chart beneath and the N is pointing north.
- Draw the line in the direction travelled as shown by the arrow on the plotter and mark the line with a **single arrowhead**.
- Mark off the distance that the boat has travelled using the difference since the last log reading.
- Mark the position with a line and write the time beside it.

It really is as simple as that. Taking a fix or plotting a GPS position can enhance

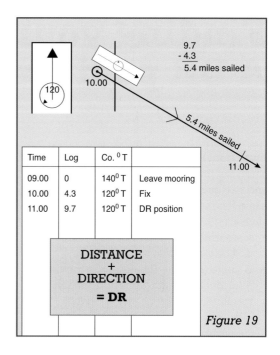

Time	Log	Co. ^{0}T	
09.00	0	140^0 T	Leave mooring
10.00	4.3	120^0 T	Fix
11.00	9.7	120^0 T	DR position

DISTANCE
+
DIRECTION
= DR

9.7
- 4.3
5.4 miles sailed

Figure 19

the accuracy of the very basic DR position. Beware of using DR position after DR position after DR position as the inaccuracies accumulate.

Plotting a DR position

1. *Set the heading in ^{0}T on the plotter.*

2. *Line up the plotter on the chart, from the last position.*

3. *Draw the course steered from the last position.*

4. *From the log, work out the distance travelled. Set the dividers to this distance, using the latitude scale.*

5. *Measure the distance along the course steered.*

6. *Mark the position with a line. Then write the time beside it.*

If the boat alters course at any time a record must be made in the logbook of:
- New heading.
- Time.
- The log reading so that the distance travelled since the last position can be calculated.

Time	Log	Co. ^{0}T	
09.00	0	140^0	
10.00	4.3	120^0	Fix
11.00	9.7	120^0	DR
11.30	12.6	120^0	alter course to 100^0
12.30	18.2	100^0	DR

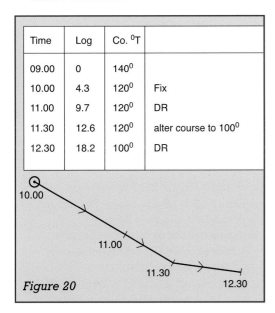

Figure 20

Traditionally, information has been written in a logbook every hour, every few hours or on every alteration of course, and the position plotted on the chart at the same time.

What about leeway?

Leeway is the effect of the wind on the boat. It is expressed as how many degrees the boat has been pushed **away** from its intended heading, perhaps 5^0, 10^0 or more. It is difficult to measure and there are no tables where you can look it up.

It varies with:
- The shape of the boat below the waterline - a long keel helps to stop sideways movement.
- The shape of the boat above the waterline - the higher the superstructure the more leeway is made.
- The speed of the boat through the water - forward speed helps to diminish the effect.
- The direction of the boat relative to the wind.

This Dehler 37 is sailing forwards nicely. But she is also making leeway towards the camera.

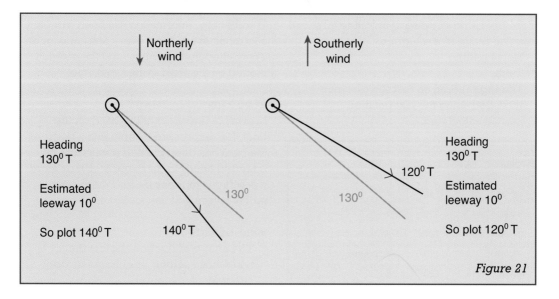

Figure 21

* And for a sailing boat...
  ...how well it is being sailed!

The skipper needs to estimate the amount of leeway that the boat is making and allow for this **before plotting on the chart**. Some people say that looking at the wake - that is watching the angle behind the boat that the wash is making and maybe taking a bearing of it with a hand-bearing compass, helps in assessing the leeway... but I am not convinced.

Estimating seems to be largely based on experience and perhaps pessimism, although GPS can now help.
The important things to remember are:
* Add or subtract the estimated leeway before plotting on the chart.
* The wind has pushed the boat **away** from the intended heading so allow the leeway **downwind** - that is, away from the wind.

ADD / SUBTRACT LEEWAY
BEFORE PLOTTING

Finding your position: 4
An Estimated Position

The DR position lacks accuracy because it does not take into account the **tidal stream** (TS). The tidal stream can be calculated and added to the diagram to give an **estimated position**.

An EP is shown like this:

How to plot an EP
- Plot the DR position.
- From the DR position draw a line that represents the direction and rate of the tidal streams that have moved the boat away from the DR position.

Time	Log	Co. ^{0} T			TS
09.00	0	140^0 T	Leave mooring		170^0 T
10.00	4.3	120^0 T	Fix		1.0 knot
11.00	9.7	120^0 T	DR position		

Tidal stream information is always given in ^{0}**T in the direction that it is going** for **each hour**. It means that the tidal stream is

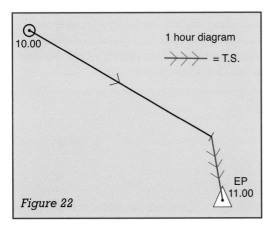

Figure 22

taking the boat 170^0 T at a speed of 1.0 knot (Figure 22). **One knot equals one nautical mile per hour.**

If the EP were for 1030 then the skipper would plot the DR position as usual, but only half the rate for the tidal steam because it would have had only half the effect (Figure 23).

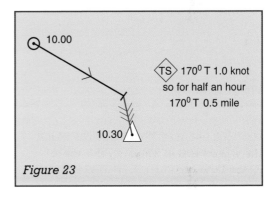

Figure 23

Always plot in that order: DR position, then tidal streams, to give an EP.

DR + TS = EP

An EP can be plotted after an hour or after several hours, if the boat is in open water.

It can be plotted if the boat has altered course, and even in the case of a yacht tacking. Plot the direction and distance sailed and then the tidal stream at the end. The important thing to remember is that the total tidal stream plotted must be in proportion to the time that the boat has been sailing. In most cases the direction and rate of the tidal stream will change from hour to hour. This is not a problem, just plot them all at the end, but remember it is only safe to do this in open water. Skippers are recommended to check their position regularly - an EP is only an estimate of position.

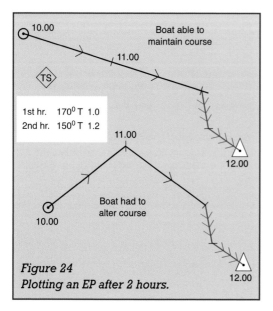

1st hr.   170⁰ T 1.0
2nd hr.   150⁰ T 1.2

Figure 24
Plotting an EP after 2 hours.

Once the plot is on the chart it shows the result of sailing in one direction while the tidal streams have been moving the boat sideways. The plot reveals how much influence the tidal streams have had on the speed of the boat and the direction of travel .

The diagram can look very different depending on the direction of the tidal stream in relation to the heading of the boat (Figure 25).

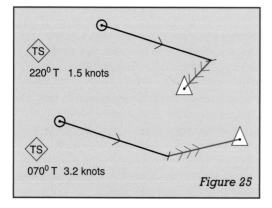

220⁰ T 1.5 knots

070⁰ T 3.2 knots

Figure 25

Course over the ground (COG)

Did the boat pass to the north or south of the buoy (Figure 26)?

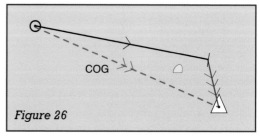

Figure 26

To the south, from the fix to the EP. The COG is shown here as a dotted line.

Speed over the ground (SOG)

Look at Figure 22 again. It shows that the boat was at the fix at 1000 and then at the EP at 1100. Although the log recorded a distance travelled of 5.4 miles the initial fix and the EP are more than 5.4 miles apart. This may look like a mistake but it is due to how the distance and speed are recorded by the log.

Most logs measure the speed and distance by means of a paddlewheel transducer mounted through the hull and show it on the display in knots (one knot equals one nautical mile per hour). As the paddlewheel spins the log measures the **speed through the water** but the log is not able to show the effect that the tidal stream is having. The tidal stream may increase or decrease the speed and the EP diagram demonstrates this. The diagram shows how quickly we are really covering the ground, it shows our **speed over the ground**, which the log is not able to do (Figure 27).

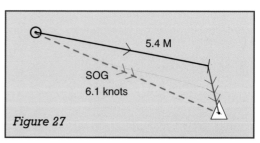

Figure 27

Without a diagram the speed over the ground is not always obvious but the difference it can make to a boat travelling at a slow speed is amazing.

This is yet another reason why it is so important for a skipper to know how the tidal streams are affecting the boat all the time: the tide's speed as well as its direction. This is especially true for skippers of relatively slow boats like yachts. On a passage along the coast, going with the tidal streams makes a huge difference for a yacht crew. Going against the tidal streams is like walking up a down escalator, it's not impossible to reach the top, but it's not quick and it's not clever.

Imagine two yachts sailing at 4 knots with a tidal stream of 2 knots. One is sailing up the coast and the other down the coast (Figure 28).

knowing about the tidal streams is still important. Planning to go **when the tidal stream is in the same direction as the wind** will give flatter water, higher cruising speed and better fuel efficiency.

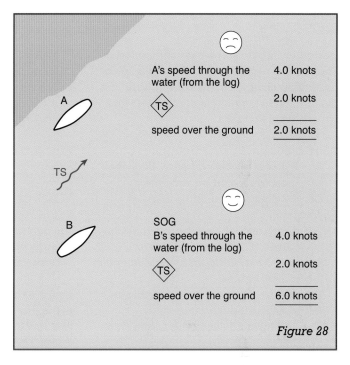

A's speed through the water (from the log)	4.0 knots
TS	2.0 knots
speed over the ground	2.0 knots

SOG B's speed through the water (from the log)	4.0 knots
TS	2.0 knots
speed over the ground	6.0 knots

Figure 28

On both boats the speed through the water is 4 knots, the log shows 4 knots on both boats. Both boats feel as if they are making the same progress, but one crew will be in the showers and the bar way ahead of the other. So don't just get up, have breakfast and go, check the tidal streams and go at the best time.

All this means that it is possible for a yacht skipper to make a passage to a port 30 miles away but for the log to show that the boat has sailed only 25 miles through the water to get there. Conversely the crew on the boat where the skipper does not plan may have to sail further through the water than the total distance on the chart. A case of 'up the down escalator'.

For a fast motor cruiser lack of speed over the ground is not so much of an issue but

GPS is especially useful again because it has the ability to calculate speed over the ground (SOG) and show it on the display. It can do this so quickly and easily because it updates its position every few seconds.

GPS showing speed through the water and speed over the ground.

A, sailing <u>against</u> a 2kn tide. *B, sailing <u>with</u> a 2kn tide.*

Looking at tides: 1 General introduction

Navigation would be so easy without tides. They cause vertical movement of the water producing changes in the **tidal height** and the horizontal movement of the water that we call **tidal streams**.

Without tides:
- An EP would be unnecessary, because a DR position would be accurate.
- Coastal passages could be made at any time.
- The direction to the next mark could be measured off the chart and steered, because the tidal streams would not push the boat off course.
- The depths over rocks and sandbanks would always be the same.
- The depth would always be as shown on the chart.
- The chart would show if there was enough water to get into a river or harbour.
- After anchoring the water level would not change. This would reduce the risk of the anchor dragging if too little

anchor cable had been laid out to allow for the rise of the tide.
- The boat could not go aground on a mooring, because the water level would not drop.

The list is enough to show that tides affect all aspects of boating.

What causes the tides?

The gravitational pull of the moon and the sun on the water causes the tides, and their relative positions in the sky produce the patterns in the behaviour of the tides.

As the earth spins throughout the 24 hours of the day we experience two high waters and two low waters, about $6^{1}/_{4}$ hours apart. The sun is sometimes pulling with the moon and sometimes against it and this leads to some high waters being much higher than others (Figure 29). This pattern of larger tides occurs fortnightly and is called **spring tides**. A spring tide has a higher high water and

Arun Yacht Club at high water...

...and at low high water.

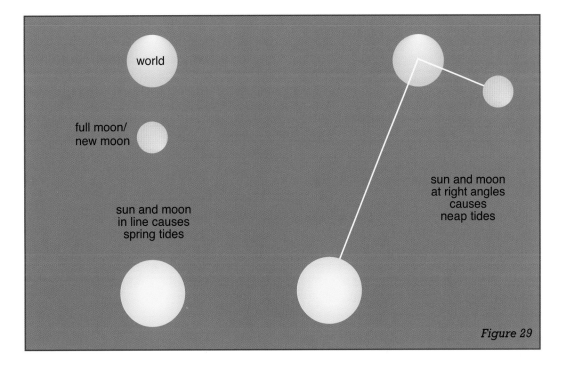

world

full moon/
new moon

sun and moon
in line causes
spring tides

sun and moon
at right angles
causes
neap tides

Figure 29

a lower low water. Between the spring tides are **neap tides** where the high water is less high and the low water less low. Spring and neap tides occur throughout the year about a week apart but how extreme they are varies too. The most dramatic spring tides of the year occur in March and September, with the Equinox.

I have heard people say "It is spring tides this week." This is as absurd as saying "It is Monday this week." Tides move gradually from neaps to springs and then back again in a natural cycle. Each day the HW is likely to be a little higher until it reaches a peak and then declines again.

As soon as the subject of tides comes up there seem to be lots of new terms and it is useful to get their meanings sorted out straight away.

Range of the tide. The range of the tide is the difference in height between HW and LW. The range is the most reliable method of calculating if it is a spring or neap tide by comparing it to the mean range for springs and neaps at the port.

> **Range = high water – low water.**

Spring tide. Spring tides occur about two days after full moon and new moon. The HW is very high and the LW very low, giving the greatest range. The tidal streams are also at their strongest, because there is more water to flow in and out but the same number of hours between high water and low water.

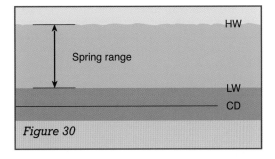

HW

Spring range

LW

CD

Figure 30

Neap tide. The HW and LW are less extreme when there is a neap tide so the

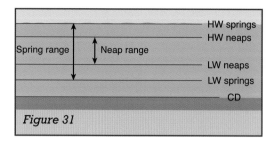

Figure 31

range is smaller. The tidal streams are weaker too.

Chart datum. Chart datum is the reference level on charts from which depths and drying heights are measured. CD is the lowest level that the water is expected to fall, under normal conditions, and is therefore the Lowest Astronomical Tide.

Drying height. A drying height is the amount a rock, mudflat or sandbank dries or sticks up above chart datum. Although it is above chart datum it is not always above the water. These are the areas on the chart shaded in green, where the numbers are underlined. Although they show so well on the chart they are not always visible to the navigator as sometimes the area will be covered by water.

Charted depth. The charted depth or **soundings** are the numbers written in black on the chart. The charted depth does not include the tide, so there is almost always more water than shown.

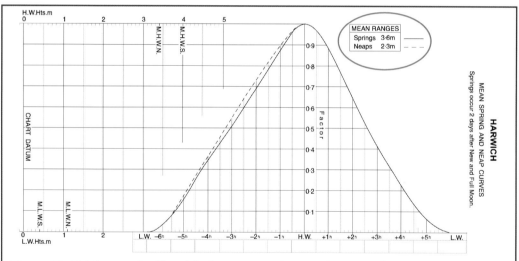

Figure 32. Tidal curve for Harwich shows mean (average) range of the tide for spring and neap tides.

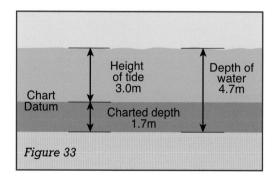

Figure 33

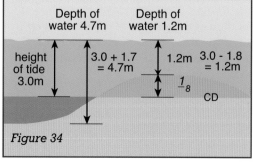

Figure 34

Height of tide. The height of tide is the amount of water above chart datum. The height of tide for high water and low water is shown in the tide tables. During the (approximately) 6 hours between high water and low water the height of tide has to be calculated on a tidal curve graph (Figure 32).

Depth of water see Figure 33). The depth of water is the amount of water from the surface to the sea bed. The depth of water can be calculated:

> **Height of tide + charted depth = depth of water**

For a drying height the depth is calculated as in Figure 34.

Rise of tide. The rise of the tide is the amount the tide has risen since low water.

Fall of tide. The amount the tide will fall until low water.

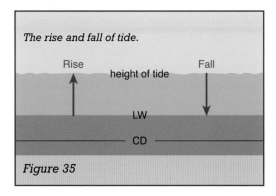

The rise and fall of tide.

Figure 35

Charted height. The charted height is the height of a lighthouse or the clearance under a bridge at MHWS. MHWS is used as the reference for these because it gives a pessimistic answer. If it is not MHWS then the tide will be lower and there will be more clearance beneath the bridge.

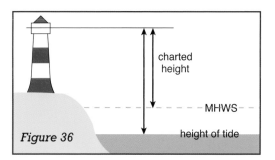

Figure 36

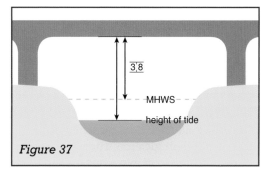

Figure 37

On the chart the elevation is shown:

3 8   meaning 38 m.

The height of a lighthouse is shown on the chart to give an indication of how far away it can be seen: the taller the lighthouse the further away it will be seen. When the tidal height is below MHWS then the lighthouse will be higher above the water and therefore visible at a greater distance. The height of eye of the observer has to be taken into account too and in the almanac there is a table to do this.

MHWS. Mean high water springs is the average height of high water for all spring tides.
MHWN. Mean high water neaps is the average height of high water for all neap tides.
MLWS. Mean low water springs is the average height of low water for all spring tides.
MLWN. Mean low water neaps is the average height of low water for all neap tides.

Looking at tides: 2 Tide tables and tidal heights

Information about tides starts with tide tables, which are produced in many forms

- Admiralty tide tables contain only tidal information. They include many national and international ports and are the size and weight of a telephone directory!
- Some marinas, chandlers and ports publish small booklets containing tide tables for their location. They are usually small enough to fit into a pocket and very useful, but only cover a small area.
- Almanacs include tidal data for many ports and also an enormous amount of other information on ports, safety matters, weather forecasts and much, much more. They are an almost essential reference book on a boat.

Whatever source is used not all the ports can be included. Those listed are known as **standard ports** and HW and LW times and heights are shown for every day of the year. Don't forget that the height given is the

height of tide, that is the amount of water above chart datum. Looking up the details for standard ports is straightforward. To use the table:
- Check the port, month and date. Look twice, as it is easy to make mistakes.
- Note the HW and LW details.
- Consider the time zone, and add an hour for daylight saving time (DST), that is BST, when required.

UK tide tables are written in UT (Universal Time), which is the same as GMT, and so from March to October an hour needs to be added to convert to British Summer Time (BST).

The time zone for the table will be printed at the top of the page. For example the time zone for France, Belgium and Holland is " – 1", meaning minus one hour. The " –1" time zone indicates than one hour needs to be **subtracted** throughout the year to convert the times in the table **back to UT**. That is how time zones are written.

In summer, of course, it is necessary to add an hour back on to convert to BST, and maybe another hour as well for local summer time. These calculations may seem complicated when planning at home but it is the same as adjusting your watch just before the plane lands.

While looking up the HW and LW in the almanac it is a good idea to take the opportunity to calculate whether the tides are on neaps or springs or somewhere in between. Some skippers

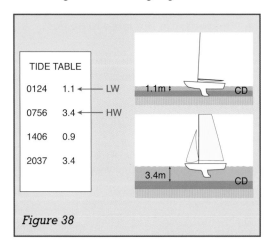

TIDE TABLE		
0124	1.1	LW
0756	3.4	HW
1406	0.9	
2037	3.4	

Figure 38

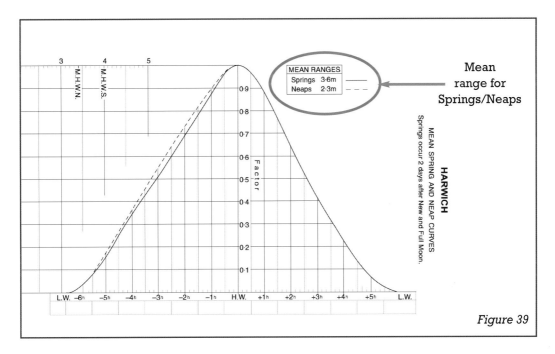

Figure 39

guess whether it is neaps or springs by scanning the list and spotting the largest HW and then assuming that it is a spring tide. It is better to calculate, and not at all complicated.

How to decide if it is springs or neaps

- Look up the HW and LW height for the day.
- Calculate the range of the tide (HW - LW).
- Compare the range of the tide that day to the mean range for the port. The mean, or average, range for the port can be found in the almanac near the tidal curve diagram, which we will look at later. Here, the mean spring range is 3.6m and the neap range is 2.3m.

Using this method to calculate between neaps and springs is quick and accurate and shows the occasions when the tides come outside the average range, affecting the strength of the tidal streams. For example, if the range is 3.8m or 4.1m, we are on 'super springs' or a big spring tide.

Secondary Ports

Anywhere that does not have a full table in the almanac is known as a Secondary Port, irrespective of the size. For these ports simple calculations have to be made to work out the time and height of HW and LW. This converts the data for the Standard Port to the Secondary Port.

The principle is very simple:

- Ports that are near to each other often have tide times that are quite similar in a regular pattern, either a bit earlier or a bit later.
- If the difference between the time of the tide at the Standard Port and the time of the tide at the Secondary Port is known, then the latter can be calculated.

Looking this up in the pocket tide tables shows the simple logic of this.

Harwich is a standard port with its own pocket tide table. On a table the differences to add or subtract from the time of HW at Harwich are listed for

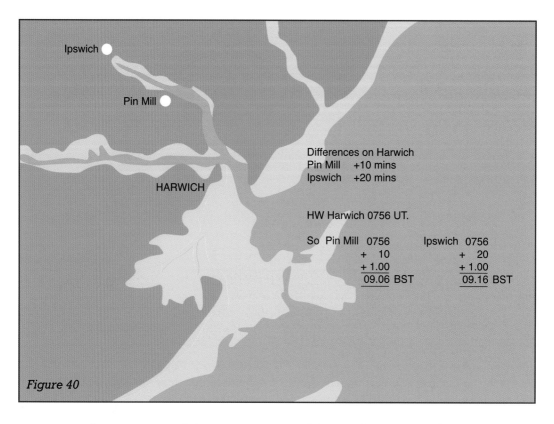

Ipswich

Pin Mill

HARWICH

Differences on Harwich
Pin Mill   +10 mins
Ipswich   +20 mins

HW Harwich 0756 UT.

So Pin Mill 0756   Ipswich 0756
              +   10   +   20
              + 1.00   + 1.00
              09.06 BST   09.16 BST

Figure 40

many secondary ports up and down the coast nearby.

For Ipswich, which is up the River Orwell from Harwich, the difference is listed as +20, meaning twenty minutes later.

For Pin Mill, the pretty riverside hamlet with the famous 'Butt and Oyster' Pub, which is half way up the river from Harwich to Ipswich, the difference is +10 or ten minutes later.

It's as simple as that, and usually quite accurate enough.

But....

There are more detailed tables in almanacs and the Admiralty tide tables that show that there is a little more to it than that.

• The adjustments shown in the pocket tables are the average of two differences given in the almanac.
• In the almanac the two differences are for springs and neaps. The pocket table might say + 20 minutes when the almanac gave +15 and + 25 minutes.
• When the differences vary a great deal, especially when it is not dead on springs or neaps, then it is necessary to look at the two figures and calculate or estimate how much to add or subtract between the two extremes (interpolate).
• In some places where the flow of water is complicated by the shape of the land, such as the Solent, the differences are complex too. This can mean that the two differences are hours apart. **Look for more information in local pilot books if the situation seems very hard to understand.** Many secondary ports that are both complex and popular publish their own pocket tide tables to save skippers complicated calculations.

How the Secondary Port table works

Standard Port	HW		LW			MHWS	MHWN	MLWN	MLWS
Harwich	0000	0600	0000	0600					
	1200	1800	1200	1800		4.0	3.4	1.1	0.4
Secondary Port	+0015	+0025	0000	+0010		+0.2	0.0	-0.1	-0.1
Ipswich									

If HW today at Harwich is 0000 UT or 1200 UT ADD 15 mins

If HW today at Harwich is 0600 UT or 1800 UT ADD 25 mins

If HW today at Harwich is 4.0 + 0.2 for HW at Ipswich

If HW today at Harwich is 3.4 add 0.0

BUT if between

0000 ⇄ 0600
1200 ⇄ 1800

ADD between 15 and 25 mins

If between 4.0 ⟶ 3.4 at Harwich today add between +0.2 and 0.0

HW Harwich	3.4
	+ 0.0
HW	**3.4m**
	at Ipswich

TODAY   0756 – call it 0800

That is between 0600 and 1200

So is between +25 and +15

but nearer 0600 so nearer 25 mins

so add about 22 minutes

0756	**UT**
+ 22	
+ 1.00	
09.18	**BST**

To make things easier it is possible to download 7 day's worth of tidal data for both Standard and Secondary Ports from www.ukho.gov.uk/easytide and there are programs for PCs.

Looking at tides: 3
Tidal streams

In some ways tidal streams seem like a different subject to tidal heights, but obviously they are not, as they are caused by the rise and fall of the tides.

Tidal streams are the **horizontal movement** of the water and they are hugely important in navigation. Some people talk of currents when they mean tidal streams. Ocean currents, like the Gulf Stream or the Equatorial Current, generally flow in a constant direction, whereas a tidal stream **changes direction**, usually near high water and low water. On average tidal streams flow for 6 hours in one direction and then for 6 hours in the other.

Generally:

- The direction of the tidal streams is along the coast.
- Tidal streams flow very strongly if the water is forced through a narrow gap between islands or at the mouth of a river.
- Tidal streams flow more strongly round headlands.
- On average the tidal streams are strongest during the 3rd and 4th hours of the 6 hour run and slackest at the turn of the tide.
- Tidal streams are less strong in the shallow water near the banks of a river or in a bay.
- Tidal streams are strongest during **spring** tides, when the range is at its greatest, because there is a greater volume of water but still just a 6 hour run.

How do navigators know what the tidal streams are doing?

In a river or when passing a fixed object like a buoy or moored boat it is often easy to **see the direction** of the tidal stream. A moored or anchored yacht will almost always lie to the tide because of its keel. If the wind is very strong and the tide very weak, or if the boat has no keel, then the direction it lies will be more influenced by the wind.

Sometimes the **strength** of the tide is dramatically obvious as well.

These anchored boats are all lying to the tide.

The 'bow wave' and wake of this buoy show the tide's direction and strength.

At sea these visual clues are rare and it is easier to forget the effect that the tidal stream is having on the boat. Ignoring the tidal stream influence when planning a passage can add hours to the journey but more dangerous is not allowing for its effect when passing fixed objects, such as a navigation buoy, or navigating past sandbanks or rocks. Skippers need to keep tidal streams uppermost in their minds and calculate them using:

- **Tidal diamonds** shown on the **chart**.
- **A tidal atlas**, which is a **book** showing the tidal streams on maps of an area.

People ask which is better, but they are just different ways of showing the same information. The atlas displays the detail in a graphic way on maps and the tidal diamonds show the information in a table of figures on the chart. The figures may give the impression of greater accuracy but that is not so. Sometimes one is more suitable for what you are trying to find out than the other, but both involve some looking up and interpolation.

Tidal diamonds

Tidal diamonds, identified by letters, are spread around the chart and the information is given in a table.

At the top of the table is shown the **reference port** for the tidal stream information on the whole chart. As you continue on your passage the next chart may have a different reference port. This is a very easy way to get things wrong, so make it a habit to always check the reference port.

Each row of information in the table is valid for an hour before or after high water and the figures show the **direction and rate** of the tidal stream at the position of the diamond. That is the direction the tidal stream is **going** in degrees True, so there is no need to allow for variation before plotting it on the chart. The rate or speed of the tidal stream is in knots, that is nautical miles per hour. The two different rates are for spring tides and neap tides, with the springs given first. This is easy to recognise as the rate at springs is stronger, because the range of the tide is greater. If the range is between spring and neap then **interpolate**.

The order of work is therefore:
- Look up the time of HW at the reference port, and convert to BST if necessary.
- Compare the range of the tide with the mean range to check if it is springs, neaps or in between.
- Calculate which hour to use.
- Look up the direction and rate of the tidal stream on the table.

Calculating which hour before or after HW to use is very important and needs to be done systematically. Just looking and guessing which hour to use, in my experience, does not produce accurate results. Obviously the tidal stream does not suddenly change direction but the information is assumed to be the average for each hour. Each direction and rate from the table is valid for the hour, so if HW is 1215, then the hour of high water is from $^1/_2$ hour before the actual time of HW to

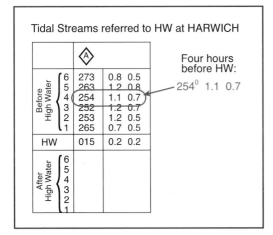

Tidal Streams referred to HW at HARWICH

		A			Four hours before HW:
Before High Water	6	273	0.8	0.5	
	5	263	1.2	0.8	254° 1.1 0.7
	4	254	1.1	0.7	
	3	252	1.2	0.7	
	2	253	1.2	0.5	
	1	265	0.7	0.5	
HW		015	0.2	0.2	
After High Water	6				
	5				
	4				
	3				
	2				
	1				

¹/₂ hour after the actual time, i.e. 1145 to 1245. This follows for all the other times too and is the standard way of calculating which hour to use. It should be followed pretty rigidly, only rounding up or down the odd minutes. Again there are several ways of writing this out but I find a table successful, even if it does look a little like writing out the times tables from school!!

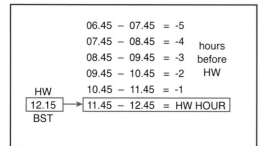

Table:

06.45 – 07.45	= -5	
07.45 – 08.45	= -4	hours
08.45 – 09.45	= -3	before
09.45 – 10.45	= -2	HW
10.45 – 11.45	= -1	
11.45 – 12.45	= HW HOUR	

HW 12.15 BST → 11.45 – 12.45 = HW HOUR

Tidal stream atlas

The Hydrographic Office publishes atlases showing tidal streams for different areas and smaller versions of the diagrams can be found in almanacs and on some charts. In the atlas are a series of 13 maps for the same area with the tidal streams shown as arrows and numbers to illustrate the direction and rate of the tidal streams for each hour. There is one map for each hour before and after high water at the reference port (Figure 41). The middle of the sequence of maps shows the tidal streams for the high water hour. The maps give a good visual image of the tidal stream direction and this makes an atlas especially good for **passage planning** round the coast and for a quick picture of the tidal streams while on passage. They can also be used where there is no convenient diamond.

The general **direction** of the tidal stream is obvious and this may be sufficient for a passage plan. If a precise direction is required for navigation then use a plotter to measure the direction from the best-placed arrow, on the correct page of the atlas (see photo opposite).

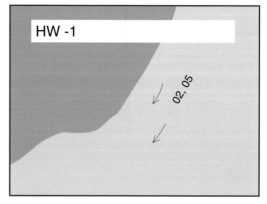

HW -1

02, 05

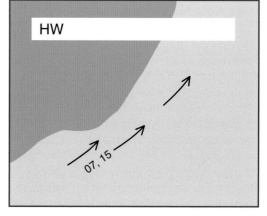

HW

07, 15

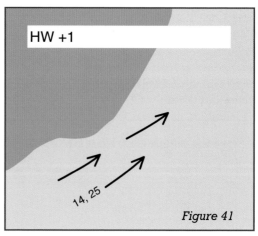

HW +1

14, 25

Figure 41

The numbers printed beside the arrows show the **rate** of the tidal streams. The two figures are the rate for spring tides and neap tides, strangely with the neaps given first this time. If you forget this it is easy to guess as the neap rate is almost always less.

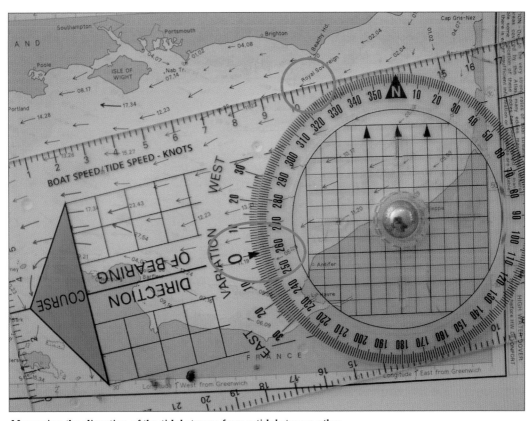

Measuring the direction of the tidal stream from a tidal stream atlas.

The numbers look a little weird as they are written without the use of a decimal point so **14, 25 means 1.4 knots at neaps and 2.5 knots at springs,** and not 14 and 25 knots! The appearance of the arrow also indicates the strength of the stream, with stronger tidal streams being shown by the darker thicker lines.

The order of work is therefore:

- Look up HW **at the reference port for the atlas** and convert to BST if necessary.
- Compare the range of the tide with the mean range to check if it is springs, neaps or in between.
- Mark up the tidal atlas, that is write on the HW page the time of HW for the reference port and then by adding and subtracting write the time on all the other pages.
Remember that **each page is valid for an hour.** That is $1/2$ hour before to $1/2$ after the exact time that you have written. Some skippers find it more convenient to write the hour that is covered on the page, rather than the exact time, to remind them of this.

Looking at tides: 4
Using tidal heights

In *Looking at tides 2* and *3* we have covered looking up the times and heights of HW and LW at standard ports and at how to convert these to secondary ports. These figures can be used with other tables or maps to calculate the tidal stream, or applied to the chart depths shown on the chart to give the depth of water:

- Charted depth + height of tide
  = depth of water
- Height of tide – drying height
  = depth of water

But.....there is more. Perhaps the plan is to go into a small harbour on a particular summer afternoon.

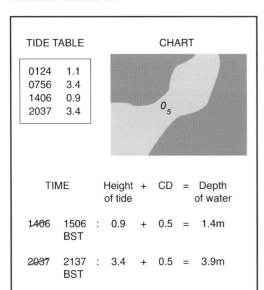

The chart shows that the charted depth is 0.5m. At 1506 BST, at LW, there will

be only 1.4m depth of water in the entrance to the harbour. Too little water to go in. At 2137, at HW, the depth of water will be 3.9m, which is plenty of water but perhaps rather late in the day for showers and dinner ashore. But if there is too little depth of water at LW and plenty at HW it must be possible to go in at some time between LW and HW as the water rises.

What time can we go in?
The answer to this question is going to be **when** there is the amount of water that we need. So the first thing to work out is how much water (or height of tide) we require.

Consider:

- The **draught** of the boat.
- The **clearance** that you want beneath the keel. This is an individual decision and may be based on the nature of the seabed, how rough the conditions are likely to be and whether the tide is rising or falling (Figures 41 and 42).
- The **information on the chart**. The charted depth or drying height.

Draught:	1.8m
Clearance:	+ 0.7m
Depth needed:	= 2.5m
Charted depth:	– 0.5m
Height of tide required:	= 2.0m

Once the height of tide required has been calculated then the **tidal curve diagram** needs to be set up (Figure 43).

From the tide table the following
information is needed:
- Time of HW. Add the hour for BST if
  necessary.

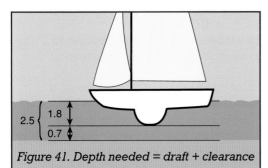

Figure 41. Depth needed = draft + clearance

*Figure 42. Height of tide required =
depth needed – charted depth*

- Height of HW.
- Height of LW.
- Spring or neap tide? This is necessary
  because in some places on the curve
  there is a different line for springs and
  neaps.

On the diagram:
1. Mark on HW and LW on the left of
   the diagram, and join them with a
   diagonal line.
2. Write the time of HW in the HW box on
   the right, beneath the curve showing
   the height of tide rising and falling,
   and fill in the other boxes as necessary
   (2137, 2037 etc).
3. Find the height of tide required,
   2.0m in this case.... draw a line
   vertically down to the diagonal
   line....draw the line horizontally
   to the curve.....then down to find
   the time. Use the neap curve or the
   spring curve or in between depending
   on the range.
4. Read off the time.....1737 + 20 minutes,
   1757 (about 6-ish) is the earliest the
   boat can go in.

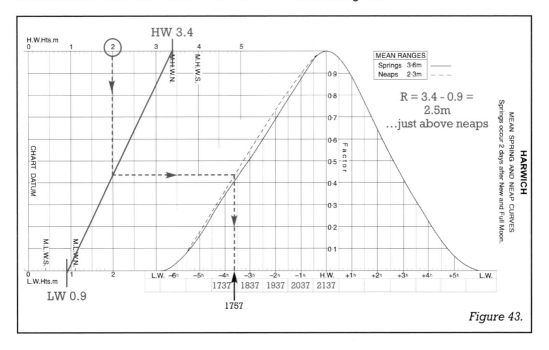

Figure 43.

Or perhaps another boat might meet this situation:

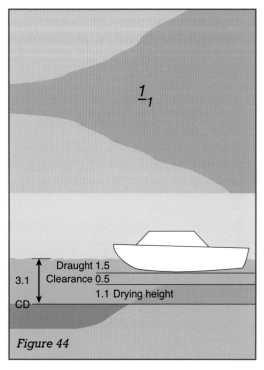

Figure 44

Draught:		1.5m
Clearance:	+	0.5m
Depth needed:	=	2.0m
Drying height:	+	1.1m
Height of tide required:	=	3.1m

The tidal curve can also be used to answer another type of question:

What is the height of tide at a specific time?

This, in a way, is the same as the last question but the other way round! The tidal curve diagram is set up in the same way using the same information as before, but using the morning HW.

- The time of HW, in BST if relevant.
- The height of HW
- The height of LW
- Springs or neaps.

What is the height of tide at 1030 BST?
1. Mark on the HW and LW and draw in the diagonal line.

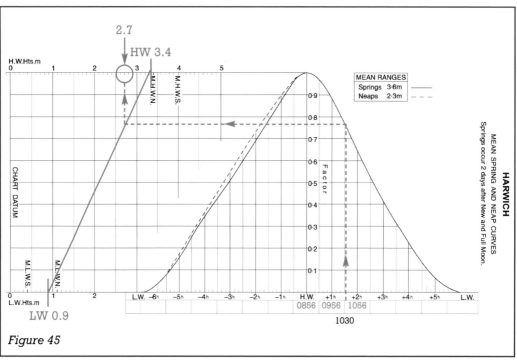

Figure 45

2. Write the time of HW in the HW box beneath the curve and fill in the other boxes as necessary

3. Find the time required …1030 in this case beneath the curve …and draw a line up to the curve …horizontally to the line …and then up to find the height of tide. Use the neap curve, the spring curve or in between depending on the range.

4. Read off the height of tide …2.7m in this case.

This type of calculation can be used when planning to anchor or moor, epecially on a falling tide.

What is the minimum depth to anchor, or for mooring?

The things to consider are:
- The **draught** of the boat.
- The **clearance** required under the keel at LW.
- The **fall of the tide** between the time of anchoring or mooring and the next LW. This is extremely easy to work out because the tide will fall from the height of tide at the time of anchoring to the level of low water. Once it is LW the tide will stop falling………
………that's why it is called low water!

> **Draught + clearance + fall**
> **= minimum depth to anchor**

The skipper decides to anchor at 1030 and realises that the tide will be falling while the boat is at anchor. It's important not to anchor in too shallow water even though this may give good shelter or keep the boat clear of other vessels, in case the vessel goes aground.

So the way to work this out is:
1. Calculate the height of tide at the time when they plan to anchor.

2. Work out how much the tide will fall while the boat is there. It will fall from its present height to the height of low water.

> **Height of tide – low water**
> **= the fall of the tide**
> **2.7m – 0.9m = 1.8m**

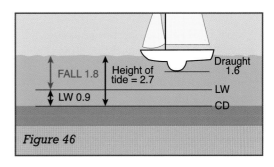

Figure 46

3. The minimum depth to anchor in at 1030 will then be:

> **draught + clearance required at LW**
> **+ the fall of the tide**
> **1.6m + 1.0m + 1.8m = 4.4m min. depth**

OR. You have picked up the only mooring available in a very popular, pretty spot but it is in quite shallow water. Will there be enough water at LW or will the boat go aground?

- Check the depth of water on the echo sounder
- Calculate the height of tide now
- Work out the fall of the tide. (Height of tide – LW)
- Don't forget the draught of the boat

> **Depth of water – fall – draught**
> **= clearance at LW**

If the place is a **secondary port**, first convert the standard port times and heights to the secondary port and then do the calculation. Use the tidal curve for the standard port if it is necessary to do a 'height of tide' calculation.

Sierra on a passage
... Pin Mill towards Brightlingsea

Sierra is preparing for the passage from Pin Mill towards Brightlingsea

Don't overload the dinghy and wear a lifejacket.

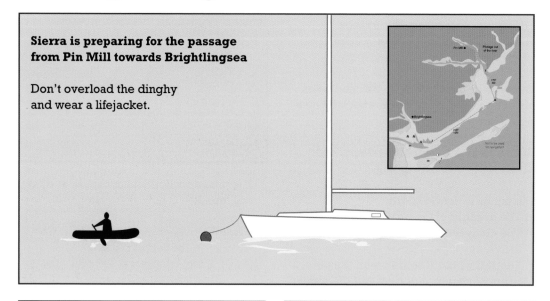

Check safety equipment and brief crew

- Lifejacket and harness
- Lifebelts/liferaft
- Flares
- Use of VHF/DSC
- Gas and fire extinguishers
- MOB procedure
- First aid kit

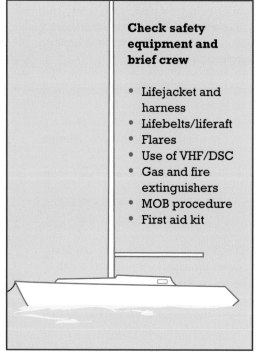

Checklist before departure

1. Charts and navigation plan
2. Engine checks
3. Sail cover off / sails ready to go
4. Weather forecast
5. Fuel/water/gas
6. All hatches shut
7. All gear stowed
8. Crew ready, waterproofs/boots/ lifejackets as necessary
9. Food prepared
10. Radar reflector up
11. Details left ashore
12. Instruments on

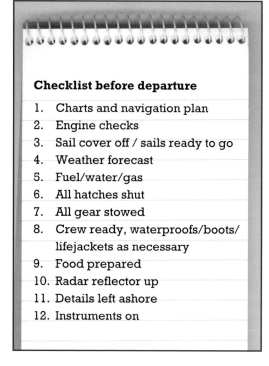

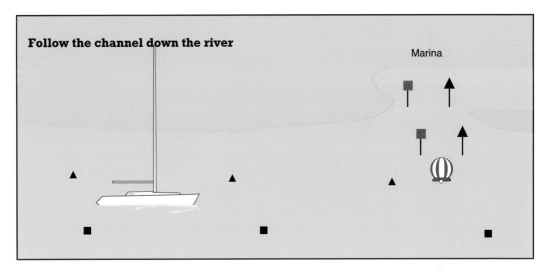

Follow the channel down the river

Marina

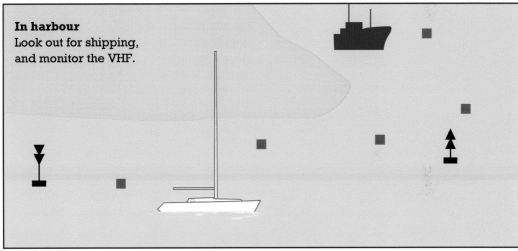

In harbour
Look out for shipping,
and monitor the VHF.

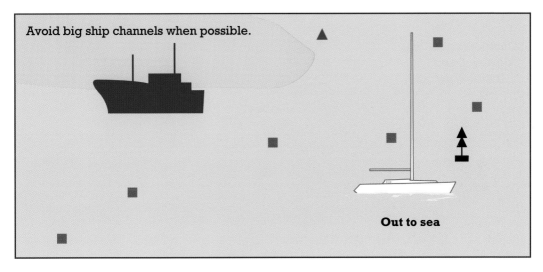

Avoid big ship channels when possible.

Out to sea

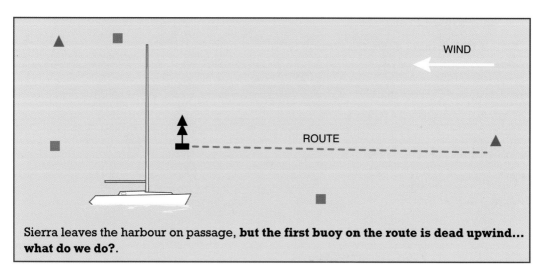

Sierra leaves the harbour on passage, **but the first buoy on the route is dead upwind... what do we do?.**

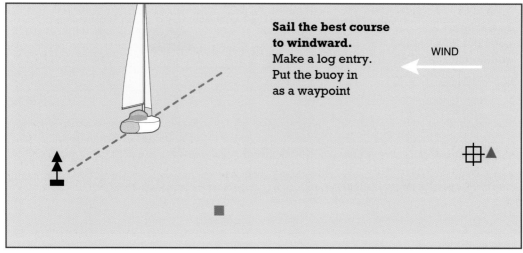

Sail the best course to windward.
Make a log entry.
Put the buoy in as a waypoint

WIND

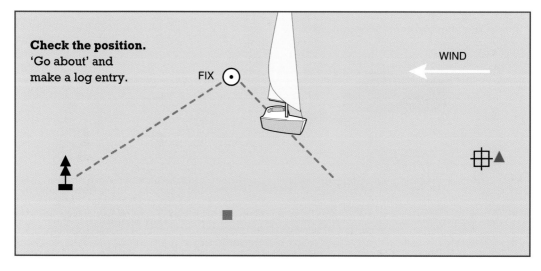

Check the position.
'Go about' and make a log entry.

FIX

WIND

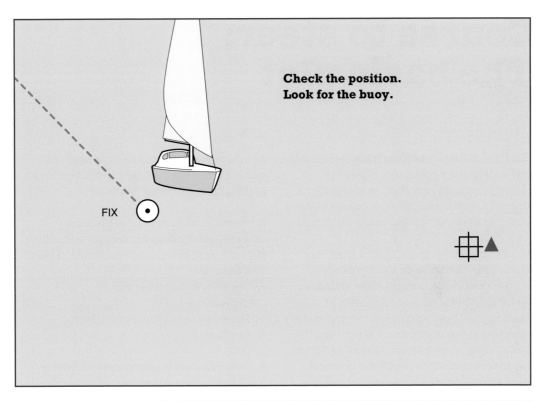

Check the position.
Look for the buoy.

FIX

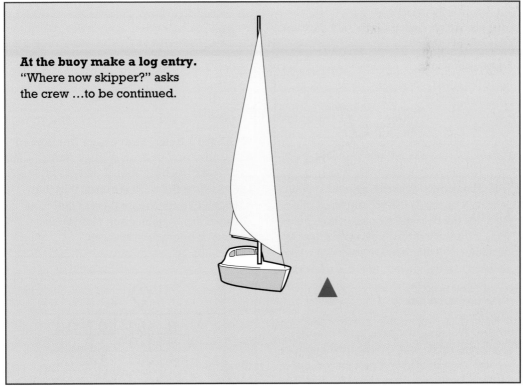

At the buoy make a log entry.
"Where now skipper?" asks
the crew ...to be continued.

Course to steer: 1
The basic plot

From the chartwork point of view calculating and understanding a course to steer is perhaps the most important and most regularly used part of navigation. A course to steer is vital, to make navigation safe and efficient.

Although at first glance the diagram may look a little similar to an EP, the purpose of the calculation is **completely different**. An EP is one of a range of methods of checking the boat's position, to answer the first question in navigation "Where am I?" GPS is used more frequently than an EP (or any other method) to check the position, because it is quick and generally reliable,

but there is only one way to answer the second question "Where should I go now?" and that is the **course to steer**.

A course to steer is unique because it involves **predicting** the course that will take the boat to a chosen position. It takes into account:
- The tidal stream that will be experienced.
- The estimated speed of the boat.
- Any leeway.

A course to steer is calculated in advance; it is a form of **pre-planning**, adjusting the

How to work out a course to steer.

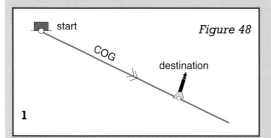

Figure 48

1

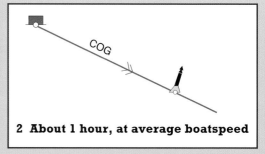

2 About 1 hour, at average boatspeed

1 **Plot the course over the ground on the chart.** This line is the ground track, the line that the boat will follow, so take care that it does not cross any hazards like shallows or rocks. Always extend the line beyond the destination to avoid mistakes in plotting at a later stage. Mark this line with two arrow heads.
2 **Estimate how long it will take to get there.** This does not have to be precise, just measure the distance to travel and use the average boat speed, working to the nearest convenient hour or half hour.

3 **Calculate the tidal streams that the boat will experience during that time.** This is pre-planning don't forget, so it must be future tidal streams.

		A		
	-6	180°	0.7	0.3
3	-5	170°	1.0	0.6
	-4	000°	1.8	1.0

way the boat is heading before setting off to prevent the tidal streams and the leeway from pushing the boat off the desired track. **A basic GPS set cannot do this.** If the destination is put into the GPS as a waypoint the set will calculate the direction towards it and keep updating that as the boat moves, but it will not take into account the tidal streams, because the set does not have that information. The boat may be pushed away from the track, possibly into a dangerous situation. Remember that GPS is a great aid to navigation but essentially it is a position-fixing device. After the skipper has calculated a course to steer the GPS can be invaluable for checking that everything is going well while the course is sailed. In fact, without GPS, if there is nothing on which to take a bearing, it can be impossible to check a course to steer. The skipper may only know that they are wrong when the buoy fails to appear!

The principal of a course to steer is easy to see when a boat is steering into the entrance of a marina where there is a strong cross-tide. The experienced helmsman can see and feel that the boat is being pushed sideways by the tidal stream and will instinctively head up into the tidal stream to compensate (Figure 47).

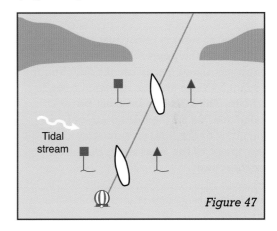

Figure 47

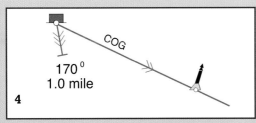

170 ⁰
1.0 mile

4

4 Plot the tidal streams from the initial position. Plot the tidal streams in the direction they are going and mark the line with three arrowheads as usual.

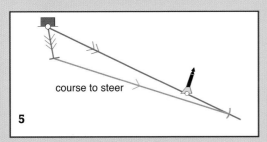

course to steer

5

5 Now the effect of the speed must be considered. Use the average speed of the boat through the water from the log. If this

is a one hour diagram set the dividers to one hour of boatspeed and mark this distance from the end of the tidal stream to the point it crosses the ground track. Draw a line from the end of the tidal stream to the point marked on the ground track. This last line is the **course to steer**. The course to steer from the chart will be in ⁰T so adjust for variation before telling the helmsman. Take great care with this last step. Do not just draw the line from the end of the tidal stream straight to the destination, it may look neat but it is wrong, and a very common plotting error.

6 Consider leeway. How much the wind may push the boat off the ground track needs to be allowed for before telling the helmsman the course to steer ...more of this later.

This order of working is reliable and with a bit of practice quite easy.

If they can see that altering the heading alone is not sufficient the experienced helmsman will increase the speed. The speed of the boat is obviously significant, especially lack of speed when the sideways effect of the tidal stream will be felt more strongly. These adjustments to the heading and to the speed are often made by eye or by following markers put up to form a **transit**.

A course to steer is really just the same, but without the posts and the narrow entrance ahead the effect of tidal stream cannot be seen and the allowance made by eye. The tidal stream must be calculated using the tidal diamonds on the chart or the tidal stream atlas and **the speed of the boat must be taken into account.**

The basic method of calculating a course to steer is very straightforward and needs to be worked out in good time, before the boat arrives at the position where the skipper intends to alter course. Once at that position the crew will ask, "What's the next course, skipper?" and the skipper needs to be ready with an answer. "Er, well I'm not sure" will not inspire them with confidence. I heard a skipper say once, "Sail round the buoy while I work it out." Not a good idea! (Figure 48, p58-9.)

Additionally, just a quick look at the finished diagram should be enough to see approximately when the boat will arrive. A rough estimated time of arrival (ETA) is quite good enough usually, and useful too. It avoids skippers worrying when they cannot see the next buoy ages before it will be

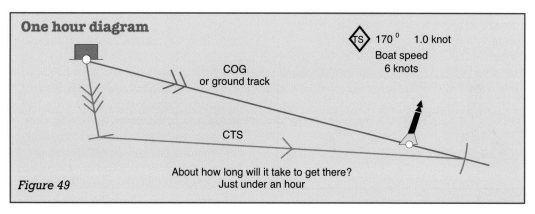

One hour diagram

TS⟩ 170 ⁰   1.0 knot
Boat speed
6 knots

COG
or ground track

CTS

About how long will it take to get there?
Just under an hour

Figure 49

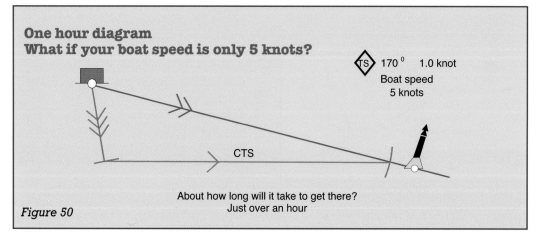

One hour diagram
What if your boat speed is only 5 knots?

TS⟩ 170 ⁰   1.0 knot
Boat speed
5 knots

CTS

About how long will it take to get there?
Just over an hour

Figure 50

visible and allows time for a cup of coffee! (See figures 49 and 50).

Many skippers plan their trip using the buoys as marks along the route. This is fine but remember that buoys can be a little off their charted position. Also, although using a buoy is convenient because it is easy to know when you have found it and the buoy gives the skipper a fix of position, be

cautious. In poor visibility or in the dark the boat could come dangerously close to a very solid object. Motor cruiser skippers often set the waypoint near, but not dead on, the buoy because of their speed.

OK, so plotting a course to steer is easy, follow the steps and you cannot go wrong so… what has gone wrong with these diagrams?

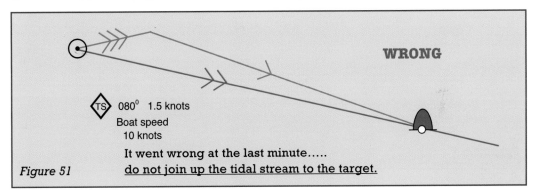

WRONG

TS 080⁰ 1.5 knots
Boat speed
10 knots

It went wrong at the last minute.....
do not join up the tidal stream to the target.

Figure 51

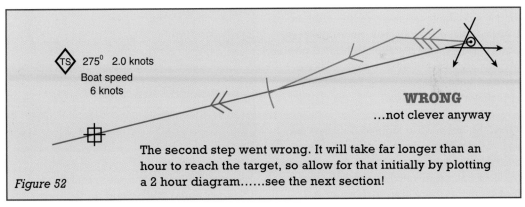

TS 275⁰ 2.0 knots
Boat speed
6 knots

WRONG

...not clever anyway

The second step went wrong. It will take far longer than an hour to reach the target, so allow for that initially by plotting a 2 hour diagram......see the next section!

Figure 52

Revision of chart plotting symbols

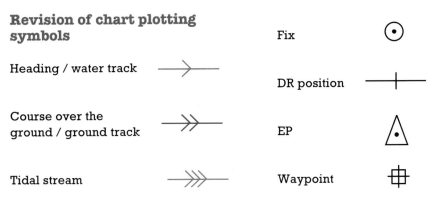

Heading / water track

Course over the ground / ground track

Tidal stream

Fix

DR position

EP

Waypoint

Course to steer: 2
...so much more

With a bit of practice calculating a simple course to steer becomes quite straightforward, but it is worth looking at the basic diagram again to see what else it shows.

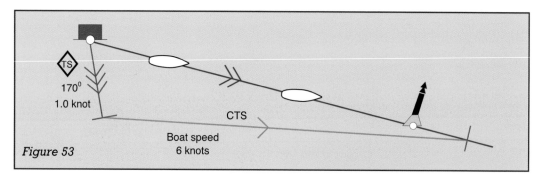

TS
170⁰
1.0 knot

CTS

Boat speed
6 knots

Figure 53

From the diagram it is easy to see about how long it will take to get there (a bit under an hour) and the crew can look out for the buoy. Don't expect to see it until it's within a couple of miles and even then what looked like a cardinal buoy can turn out to be a yacht with tan sails as you get closer!

When the buoy is first sighted the crew may say, "I can see the buoy skipper. It's way over there", pointing perhaps 20⁰ or 30⁰ off the bow (their tone of voice implying that they think that there is something wrong). "Shall I just aim at the buoy?" the helmsman may ask, trying to be helpful.

To agree could be a mistake. When looking for the next buoy in a river or at sea there seems to be a natural tendency to look dead ahead, to expect what we are looking for to turn up straight in front. In a cross-tide situation this will never be the case. The point of calculating the course to steer in advance is to allow for the tidal stream that will push the boat away from the desired course over the ground. When the course to steer is

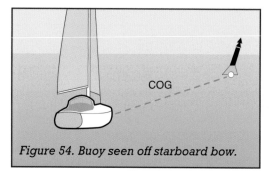

COG

Figure 54. Buoy seen off starboard bow.

followed the boat is therefore crabbing sideways along this ground track. Taking another look at the diagram will make it clear whether to expect the buoy to be on the port bow or the starboard bow.

Just as no skipper should jump to the conclusion that the course to steer is wrong because the buoy is not dead ahead, they should not assume they are right either. In fact don't assume anything. Check. There are several ways of confirming that all is well:

- If the course to steer has been calculated from a buoy, it should remain visible for at least 15 to 20 minutes to a yacht skipper, and a **back bearing** can be taken of it (Figure 55) with a hand-bearing compass. The advantage of using the buoy the boat has just left is the positive identification. The single bearing will not give a fix of position of course but it should be a reciprocal of the course over the ground that the boat is trying to achieve. If the tidal stream is not as predicted or if something else is pushing the boat off the ground track, the back bearing will show if the boat is to the right or left of the track.

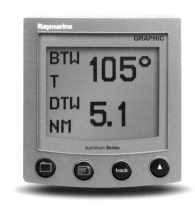

GPS showing direction and distance to the waypoint.

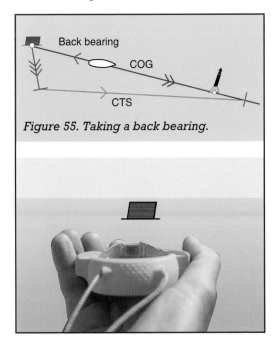

Figure 55. Taking a back bearing.

The direction shown **will not** be the same as the calculated course to steer but **will** be the same as the course over the ground and should remain reasonably constant, thus providing an excellent check.

- GPS sets have an additional feature that can help here too. This is known as the **cross track error**, often abbreviated to XTE, which shows how much the boat has been swept off the original direction to the waypoint given by the GPS. XTE is displayed as tenths of a mile away from the original direction. If the course is working perfectly the XTE will be zero, but perhaps it is more realistic to expect it to be extremely small if all is well (Figure 56).

- The north cardinal buoy ahead can be put into the GPS as a **waypoint** as a check, taking great care to measure the latitude and longitude and enter it correctly into the GPS. Mistakes at this point are some of the easiest to make! The GPS **cannot** work out the course to steer to allow for the tidal stream or leeway but it will display the direction and distance to the waypoint, updating every few seconds.

- Once the buoy is sighted and positively identified then it is easy to check that the course is going to work out. Take a bearing of the buoy with the hand-bearing compass and (once adjusted for variation), this should be the same as the course over the ground. Alternatively, take several bearings of the buoy. If they remain constant the boat is going towards the buoy.

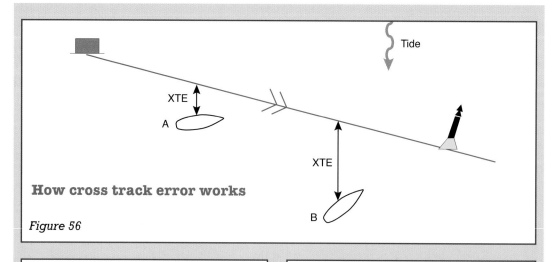

How cross track error works

Figure 56

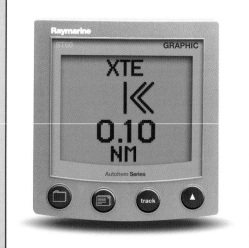

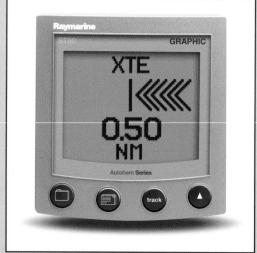

At position A the GPS shows a cross track error of 0.1 miles and tells us to turn to port. But we are swept further off course and at position B the XTE is 0.5 miles.

Leeway

If the courses are not working out well the boat may be making **leeway**. In the case of a course to steer the leeway does not appear in the diagram on the chart at all. **After** the course has been calculated assess the strength of the wind and the likely amount of leeway. Then the helmsman should **'head up'** into the wind the extra 5^0, 10^0 or more (as necessary) to prevent the wind pushing the boat off the desired course over the ground (Figure 57).

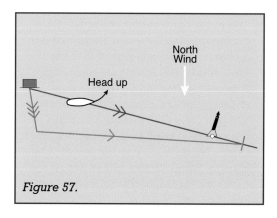

Figure 57.

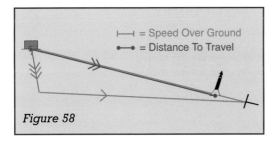

Figure 58

ETA (Estimated Time of Arrival)

In the first section we saw that it was easy to look at the diagram and predict whether it would take more or less than an hour to get to the buoy. If the skipper needs a more precise answer then it is possible to calculate that too, both from the diagram and from the GPS if the destination has been put in as a waypoint.

- On the diagram (Figure 58) measure the distance to travel and the speed over the ground.

$$\frac{\text{Distance to travel}}{\text{Speed over ground}} \times 60 = \frac{\text{Time to}}{\text{destination}}$$

$$\frac{\text{DTT}}{\text{SOG}} \times 60 = \text{ETA}$$

- The GPS will calculate the TTG (time to go) to the waypoint. As the GPS recalculates its position every few seconds, it will update the TTG so the GPS will never be wrong!

Course to steer for more or less than an hour

If, at the first stage of planning a

course to steer, it is obvious that it will *not* take about an hour to get there then adapt the diagram accordingly. In a fast boat it may be more convenient to draw a half hour diagram instead, using half the speed of the tidal stream and half the boat-speed. In the case of a diagram for less than an hour the answer will remain the same as long as the correct proportion is maintained between the speed of the tidal stream and the speed of the vessel. (See Figure 59.)

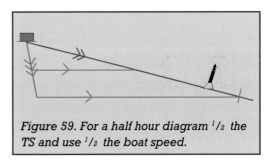

Figure 59. For a half hour diagram $^1/_2$ the TS and use $^1/_2$ the boat speed.

If it will take much longer than an hour to get to the destination **plot all the tidal stream at the beginning** (Figure 60). Look in the tidal atlas to see which tidal streams to use along the course over the ground. It is more efficient to plot all the tidal streams at the beginning because the boat will travel a shorter distance than if the boat keeps changing course. But the boat will be pushed off the ground track so it is important that skippers check that this will be safe.

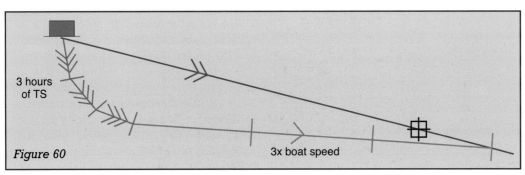

3 hours of TS

3x boat speed

Figure 60

Pilotage: 1
The buoyage system

Everyone onboard needs to be familiar with the local buoyage system. The chart will show whether the area is IALA Region A or Region B. IALA, the International Association of Lighthouse Authorities, sets the world-wide systems and standards. The USA, and countries nearby, are region B, everywhere else is Region A.

Buoys are shown on the chart as very small pictures of themselves, major lights and lighthouses are shown as stars and beacons as a combination of the two.

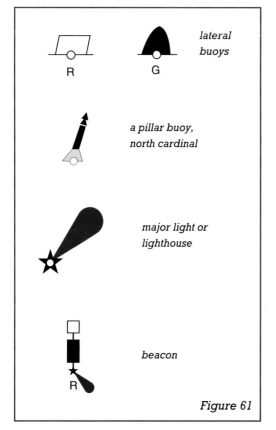

lateral
buoys

R   G

a pillar buoy,
north cardinal

major light or
lighthouse

beacon

R

Figure 61

The magenta shaped teardrop beside the image shows that the buoy is lit. No teardrop means no light. The direction that the teardrop points is insignificant. Beside each lit buoy, beacon and lighthouse are the abbreviations giving the details of the light's pattern.
The details are shown in order:
* Pattern of flashing.
* The number of flashes.
* The colour. If no colour is shown, then the light is white.
* The time period for the total pattern of the light.....i.e. the time for one cycle.
* Height of the light in meters above MHWS for beacons and lighthouses.
* The nominal range in miles. This does not mean that it can be seen at the distance shown from the flybridge or the cockpit. How far a light can be seen depends on the height and brightness of the light, the height of eye of the observer and the weather conditions at the time. The nominal range is to indicate the brightness of a light.

The list of possible **light patterns** is quite long.

F... for a fixed, that is non-flashing light. These are most commonly used on the ends of piers and jetties e.g. **2FR (vert)** or **2FG (vert)**, meaning 2 fixed lights in red or green displayed vertically. It is important to recognise these as different from the flashing light seen on a buoy or beacon. Often it is a good idea for a small vessel to pass the 'wrong' side of a navigation buoy in a busy shipping area, if there is sufficient water, to keep out of the way of commercial ships. It is obviously unsafe to pass the other side of a feature marked with fixed lights because the light is attached to the land!

Fl... for flashing e.g. Fl (2) with the number of flashes always shown in brackets.

LFl... for long flash

Q... for quick flash or VQ for very quick flash.

Iso... for isophase, meaning equal periods with the light on and the light off

Oc... for occulting. This is similar in a way to flashing, but the other way around. With a flashing light the light is basically off and then comes on for short periods. Occulting is the opposite with the light being on and then going off for short periods. It was once described to me as "flashing darkness", which made sense to me!

Mo... for a Morse flashing light, as in **Mo (A) or Mo (U)**

Colour is shown with easily-guessed abbreviations.

R... for red

G... for green

Y... for yellow

These are the most common, but **Bu** and **Or** are also used for blue and orange. The same letters are used below the buoy or beacon to show the colour of the structure.

This all fits together in a set order with the total time period in seconds at the end, for example 5s or 10s. Remember that this is the period before the sequence is repeated, not the period of darkness.

Here are a few to practise decoding. (The answers are at the end of the section.)
a) Fl (2) 20s 12m 24M on a light vessel
b) VQ (6) + LFL 10s
c) Mo (U) 15s 2m 3M on a beacon
d) Fl. Y 2.5s
e) Iso. 10s
f) Oc. (2) WR 15s 10m 18M on a lighthouse where the sector of visibility of the red and white light is shown on the chart. The sector is the area, or areas, where the light is visible. The sectors are marked on the chart and help to guide vessels into a narrow harbour or protect them from hazards like rocks (see Figure 62).

A sequence that that cannot be decoded can be found in the book 5011, Symbols and Abbreviations used on Admiralty Charts.

Types of buoys and beacons

Generally these fall into three types

- **Lateral marks** which are red or green
- **Cardinal marks,** which are black and yellow.

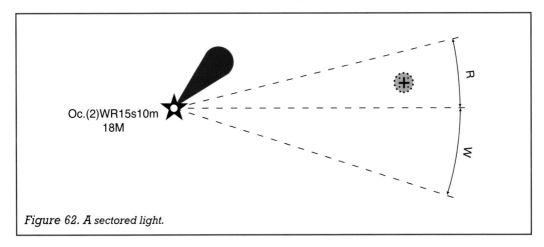

Figure 62. A sectored light.

- **Other marks** which are used as necessary. These include: **special marks** which are yellow; **safe water marks** which are red and white; **isolated danger marks** which are red and black.

Lateral Marks

These mark the channel and show where the deepest water is located, but do not neccessarily mean that it is deep enough for the boat at all states of the tide.

Large shipping channels may be so deep that there is room to navigate just outside the channel. In some ports small boats are required to do this under local regulations. Details will be found in the almanac. Lateral marks are often called port hand and starboard hand buoys, but there is more to it that that. Whether the skipper should leave then to port or starboard depends on whether the boat is going into or out of the river and if the plan is to follow just inside or just outside the channel. So maybe it is easier to call them red and green buoys or beacons. **For IALA Region A, if coming in from the sea then red buoys should be left to port and green buoys to starboard to be in the marked channel** (Figure 63).

The light characteristics of red and green buoys are straightforward. All red buoys flash red and all green buoys flash green, if they are lit.

Some very small channels are marked by withies, which are willow sticks driven into the mud or sand, or by small buoys placed by yacht clubs.

Cardinal buoys and beacons

The common diagram of the four cardinal buoys round the danger gives the impression that every hazard is surrounded with buoys, but in reality this is not the case. A sandbank several miles long may only have a buoy every few miles. Good navigation, not buoyage, is the secret to avoiding hidden hazards.

The cardinal buoys were devised more recently so to learn them look for the logic in the shape, the colours and the light patterns.

The buoys are labelled north, south, east and west to guide the helmsman which way to pass them. **So pass north of a north cardinal, south of a south**

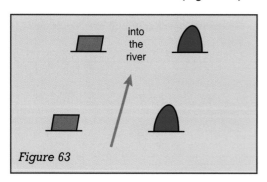

Figure 63

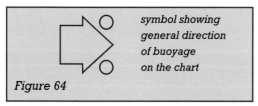

symbol showing general direction of buoyage on the chart

Figure 64

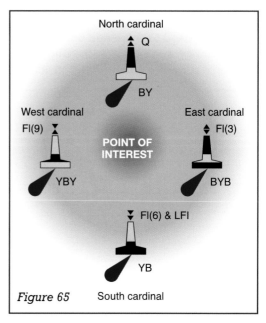

Figure 65   South cardinal

cardinal etc. The shape of the topmark on each buoy is the easiest part to learn for most people, especially with north pointing up and south pointing down, and with the east and west described as looking like an egg and a wine glass perhaps. Unfortunately the topmarks may be easy to learn but they are not that easy to see at a distance so learn the colour scheme of the buoys as well. This is simpler if you notice the pattern: the black on the buoy follows the points on the cones. For example, the cones point up on the north cardinal and the black on the buoy is on the top. This works with them all, even the east and the west.

Then there are the lights to learn. The colour is easy when you know that **all red buoys have red lights, all green buoys have green lights and all yellow buoys have yellow lights. All the rest have white.** The number of flashes shown applies to all cardinal buoys and they can be counted going round as on a clock face, with north doing a continual flash, east flashing three times, south flashing six times (with an additional long flash) and the west flashing nine times.

Other buoys

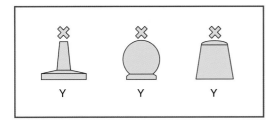

The **special mark** is yellow and has no navigational significance. Special marks may be racing buoys, or be used to indicate waterski areas, anchorages, or for other general purposes. The shape can vary but the light is always yellow, if the buoy is lit.

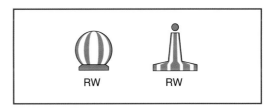

A **safe water mark** is used to mark the beginning of a buoyed channel and has red and white vertical stripes. The characteristic of the light can be L.Fl , Oc, Iso or Mo (A) and it is always white.

The **isolated danger mark** shows a hazard with safe water all around. The colour is red and black in horizontal stripes and the white light is Fl (2). The characteristic of the light is easy to remember: just look at the topmark.

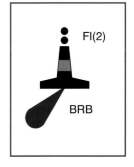

Answers:
a) Flashing twice within 20 seconds. The light is 12 meters above MHWS and has a nominal range of 24 miles.
b) This is a south cardinal buoy. It is flashing a white light very quickly 6 times followed by a long flash. The cycle is 10 seconds.
c) A white light flashing the morse letter U, that is . . - , every 15 seconds. The beacon is 2 meters above MHWS and has a nominal range of 3 miles.
d) A yellow buoy flashing a yellow light every 2.5 seconds.
e) A white light showing isophase every 10 seconds, than is on for 5 seconds and then off for 5 seconds.
f) A light red or white light, depending on the sector from which it is viewed, which is on and then goes off twice within 15 seconds. The light is 10 meters above MHWS and has a nominal range of 18 miles.

Pilotage: 2
The plan

Pilotage is quite different from navigation, because it is largely visual. In rivers and other areas that we know well it is relaxing and enjoyable; we know where we are and appreciate the hazards, in fact they aren't hazards because we are aware of them. When exploring a new area never under-estimate the difficulties of the pilotage, especially at night. It's like turning off the motorway into a town that you have never been to before: too many signs, too many side turnings, too may decisions… and instantly you're lost!

It is the part of the passage when the boat is in a confined area, the water may be shallow or there may be dangerous rocks close by. Decisions have to be made quickly and it may come at the end of a long and tiring day. Detailed navigation down below at the chart table is just too slow and takes the skipper away from the deck. It is vital to be on deck, not steering but monitoring the progress of the vessel and everything that is happening round it. There is no time to plot the GPS position or take a fix, no time even to look at the chart for more than a few moments at a time so the skipper needs to prepare a **pilotage plan**.

A few things to consider:
- The more people on board who can identify the different buoys, by light as well as shape and colour, the easier it will be. At night, with background lights, buoys can be difficult to spot so **get everyone to help**.
- Make sure you have a **detailed chart**, with up-to-date buoyage.
- It may be necessary to give the helmsman a **heading** to the next buoy if it is difficult

to see, so have this information in your plan. Tell them which side of a buoy they should pass and what effect the tidal stream is having on the boat. At night tell them how far away it is too, but don't tell them about the next two or three buoys ahead. It's hard to remember lots of details, especially if you haven't seen the chart.
- Keep things simple and in a yacht use the **engine**.
- The **almanac** will usually give the most up-to-date information because they are reprinted annually, including local regulations and port entry signals.
- Monitor the harbour **VHF** channel for information on shipping movements. Check if you need to get permission over the VHF to enter the harbour.
- The local **pilot book** will give advice on marinas, moorings and anchorages, sometimes including pictures or aerial photographs of the features described.
- Consider the **depth of water**. It may not be possible to enter the river, harbour or marina at all states of the tide.
- Have a contingency plan in case you arrive too early, too late or it is too dark or too rough to go in.
- Are there enough **lit buoys** to make it a safe area to navigate in the dark? Remember that unlit buoys, or 'blind buoys' as they are called, could be a hazard.
- Monitor the **speed** over the ground. During the day this is quite easy by general observation, at night the GPS is especially useful for this. In the dark it is easy to forget the effect that the tidal streams are having on the boat. The boat

may be travelling much faster than indicated on the log. But if you're going too slowly the boat will be more affected by any cross-tide.

- Know what the **tidal stream** is doing. Besides increasing or decreasing the speed over the ground it may be having a sideways effect on the boat pushing it towards shallow water.
- Have a **hand-bearing compass** ready and use back bearings and clearing lines to check the boat is in a safe position.
- The **echosounder** and its **alarms** can be very useful for shallow and deep water. Use them because it is impossible to watch the display all the time. If you are following a buoyed channel, especially at night, set the shallow water alarm as high as possible so that it just does not go off. This will then give an early warning if the boat begins to drift out of the channel, rather like the rumble stripes beside the motorway. They warn the driver that the vehicle is drifting onto the hard shoulder, not that they are just about to go into the ditch. Don't set the alarm for 2.0m, that could be too late, set it high to give a warning in good time.
- The deep water alarm can be used to warn that the vessel is drifting into the deep water channel. In a busy commercial harbour it may be best to keep out of this channel (if possible) and it may even be a local regulation
- **Pre-plan the route.** Draw a plan that works for you, including the buoys and lights to look out for and choose a good **starting point**. Some ports have a safe water mark in the approach as a good starting point, if not pick your own. You need to know where you are when you start.
- It is OK to follow the buoys but take one at a time, like stepping stones, and don't assume the one in the distance is the one you are looking for. Know the direction from one to the next and take care not to miss one out and cut a corner by mistake.

- At night be cautious using extra lights as they will ruin your **night vision**. The instruments on deck and the chart table light need to be usable, but not dazzling.
- A small **torch** may be necessary to read the plan on deck. Remind the crew not to use other lights down below.
- Only use a spotlight on deck if it is essential, because they are so dazzling.

There are one or two quick navigation techniques that are particularly useful for pilotage, with its need for simplicity and speed.

Transits and leading lines

Some small rivers and harbours have put up posts, other marks or lights to act as transits and show a leading line. These will be shown on the chart or described in the pilot book. The pilot book may even include a picture of what to look for. If the two objects or lights are kept in line, ahead or astern, then the boat is on the leading line.

Leading lines.

Turn to port to line them up.

Keep in line.

Figure 66

It is possible to use the same method by looking at an object, perhaps the next buoy, in relation to the background behind it. Heading the boat to keep the background behind it stationary forms a transit and will work the same way (see Figure 67).

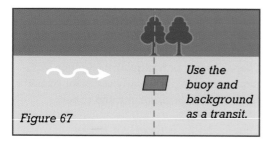

Figure 67   Use the buoy and background as a transit.

Back bearings

A back bearing works very well in pilotage, especially if there is a cross-tide. It shows if the boat is on track, or off-track to the right or left. Calculate in advance which way to turn if the back bearing shows that the boat is off-track.

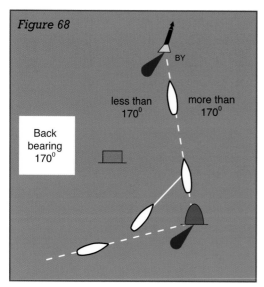

Figure 68

BY

less than 170⁰   more than 170⁰

Back bearing 170⁰

Problem:

The route into the harbour is easy in daylight, but at night there are two hazards:

1. Being dangerously close to the green buoy, the turning point for the harbour.
2. Turning to avoid the green buoy too soon and hitting the red unlit buoy which is

close to the track.

Solution:

Turn early to avoid the green buoy. Take bearings on it to check that the boat is safe. When the bearing is 170⁰ turn onto the new heading. Keep checking the back bearing: if it becomes more than 170⁰ turn to port; if less than 170⁰ , turn to starboard.

GPS waypoint

Placing a GPS waypoint in a river entrance and monitoring the Cross Track Error can be used in a similar way. Draw in the track, distance and XTE like a ladder (Figure 69). In this case there does not need to be a charted object on which to take the bearing.

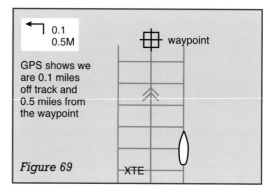

0.1
0.5M

waypoint

GPS shows we are 0.1 miles off track and 0.5 miles from the waypoint

Figure 69   XTE

Waypoint web

This pattern takes a little time to draw on the chart but it shows immediately the approximate position (Figure 70).

This is useful for navigating at speed using a laminated chart on deck.

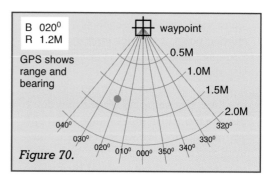

B 020⁰
R 1.2M

waypoint

GPS shows range and bearing

0.5M
1.0M
1.5M
2.0M

040⁰   320⁰
030⁰   330⁰
020⁰ 010⁰ 000⁰ 350⁰ 340⁰

Figure 70.

Clearing lines

One or two clearing lines can be used to keep the boat clear of hazards that cannot be seen. The line is drawn to mark the safe side or safe sector and by checking the bearings the skipper will know that the boat has not crossed those lines.
To be in the safe sector the bearing on the red buoy must be:

- Not more than 020°
- Not less than 340°

(See Figure 71.)

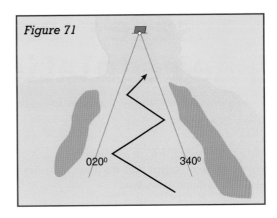

Figure 71

The Plan

This can be in the form of a list, an 'AA style' route map or an artistic sketch as suits the situation and the skipper best. I've seen them all work successfully. In the case of the sketch map take care with scale and direction so as not to build in false impressions.

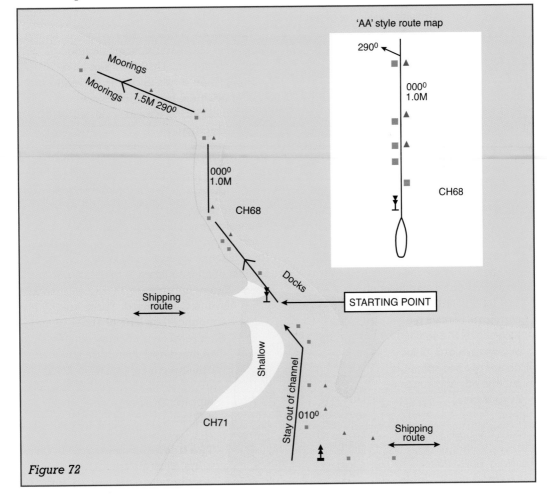

Figure 72

Passage planning: 1
The regulations

Thankfully, when we go boating there are not many regulations that we need to know about, but there are a few:

- If you have a VHF/DSC or any VHF radio on the boat then a **Ship's Radio Licence** is required. To get this contact Ofcom via their website on www.ofcom.gov.uk. The licence comes in the form of a 'tax disc' to display on the boat and a licence document to keep with the ship's papers. With this licence the boat will be given an international call-sign and an MMSI number to be programmed into the VHF/ DSC set.

- In addition at least one member of the crew must hold the appropriate **certificate** which is either the old VHF licence in the case of a basic VHF set or the SRC (Short Range Certificate) if the set is VHF/DSC. In reality it makes sense for all the crew to be competent to use the radio for both routine and emergency communications. To help with this an emergency radio procedure card can be fixed up by the set. To learn radio procedures and take the simple test for the SRC certificate contact the RYA* on 0845 345 0400 or www.rya.org.uk for details of a sea school or college offering courses in your area.

Reading *VHF Afloat* will help as well!

- **SOLAS V regulations** came into force in July 2002 and affect us all, whatever the size of the cruising boat. These regulations are part of Chapter V of the International Convention for the Safety of Life at Sea, most of which applies to large commercial vessels.

The regulations affect passage planning and safety .

1 Passage planning

The rules state that all trips should be pre-planned. This does **not** have to be written down and then submitted to the authorities, but skippers are recommended to consider the following before departing:

The weather Check the forecast before you go and get regular updates during a longer passage. For local trips over a day or weekend this is quite easy. Television, radio and the internet give good information and many marinas pin up the local inshore forecast on a notice-board. Easiest of all is to listen to the Maritime Safety Information Broadcasts made by the Coastguard. These are announced on VHF channel 16 and then read on a working channel. The times and channels used are published in the almanac. For forecasts covering a wider area the shipping forecast is available on BBC radio or via a navtex receiver.

The tides Plan the trip to fit the tides. This means taking into account the tidal heights for going into and out of marinas and harbours and when the tidal streams will be most favourable.

The limitations of the vessel The boat and its equipment must be suitable for the planned voyage. How rough the passage is going to be is determined by the strength of the wind, the distance from the sheltered shore, the length of time the wind has been blowing in the same direction and the depth of the water. Consider how the conditions will affect your boat in particular. A Force 4 or 5 will be a very different experience on an 18 foot as opposed to a 45 foot boat. The shape and type of the craft and the direction of travel in relation to the wind will all make a huge difference too.

The ability of the crew ...and skipper The plans need to be realistic for the skipper and the crew. They need to enjoy the trip, not just survive it. Passages that are too long or where the crew become ill will reduce their enthusiasm for the next trip! They need to be well prepared with warm, waterproof clothes or sun cream and hats as necessary. There needs to be lots of food easily available, and suitable for the conditions. Never lie to your crew. If it might be a bit rough then say so, explain how long it will last and the measures that you have taken to make it safe and exciting.

Don't just consider if the crew are up to the passage, but yourself as well if you are the skipper. Be honest with yourself and don't be pushed into making the trip because you said you would. If you don't fancy the forecast or you don't feel ready for the passage, then don't go. Or maybe prepare well, go and have a look, and if the conditions at sea are not nice, turn round and have a relaxing evening somewhere else. Don't forget that with a weekend trip everyone will probably need to get back the next day, so check the outlook in the weather forecast as well.

The navigation dangers in the area Make sure than in the plan potential hazards have been taken into account. These could include rocks and sandbanks, large ships, fishing vessels and fishing pots, areas of rough water or overfalls, naval activity from a firing range or submarine exercise area or a major shipping lane.

A back-up plan Always have a contingency plan. What to do and where to go if the conditions deteriorate or the crew becomes too tired, cold or seasick to want to go on, or when you arrive at the marina or river it is too late, too dark, too rough or too shallow to go in. It may be possible to divert to another port, it may be necessary to turn back or anchor.

Leaving details ashore Let someone know where you are going and when you will be back and join the Coastguard Voluntary Safety Identification Scheme (often called the CG66). To join, contact the local Coastguard station or log on to www.mcga.gov.uk.

All this is extremely good common sense and should not be considered a burden. With experience and for short trips much of this planning will become automatic and could be done in the skipper's head, but a few written notes are a good idea so the crew can get involved.

2 Radar reflectors

All vessels are required to fit a radar reflector, if practicable, as high as possible. Large ships rely heavily on radar and without a radar reflector small boats may not be seen. The radar reflector is a passive device that does exactly as it says....it reflects the radar signals of other vessels to make the boat more visible on their screen.

Life-saving signals There should be a table of life-saving signals on the boat to help the skipper and crew recognise signals used by vessels in distress. This shows the red and orange distress flares and other signals as well. An illustrated table of these signals is shown below. Any sightings should be reported to the Coastguard.

LIFE SAVING SIGNALS

To be used by Ships, Aircraft or Persons in Distress, when communicating with life-saving stations, maritime rescue units and aircraft engaged in search and rescue operations.

Maritime and Coastguard Agency

Shore to Ship Sign

Safe to land here.

Vertical waving of both ar

Landing here is dang

Horizontal waving of whi
flag, light or flare on grou
indicates direction of safe

Search and Rescue Unit Replies

You have been seen, assistance will be given as soon as possible.

OR

Orange smoke flare.

Three white star signals or three light and sound rockets fired at approximately 1 minute intervals.

Surface to Air Signals

Note: Use International Code of Signals by means of lights or flags or by laying out the symbol on the deck or ground with items which have a high contrast to the background.

Message	ICAO/IMO Visual Signals
Require assistance	V
Require medical assistance	X
No or negative	N
Yes or affirmative	Y
Proceeding in this direction	↑

Air to Surface Rep

Message Understoo

Drop a message.

Message Not Under

Straight and level f

Air to Surface Direction Signals

Sequence of 3 manoeuvres meaning proceed to this direction.

1

Circle vessel at least once.

2
Cross low, ahead a vessel rocking wings.

3

Overfly vessel and head in required direction.

Your assistance is no longer required.

Cross low, astern of vessel rocking wings.

Note: As a non preferred alternative to rocking wings, varying engine tone or volume may be used.

Surface to Air Rep

Message Understoo

Change course to required directi

I am unable to comp

Note: Use the signal most appr
to prevailling conditions,

3 Assistance to other craft

If the skipper or crew see a hazard to navigation, such as a damaged or unlit buoy, or if a distress signal is sighted or a life-belt found a report should be

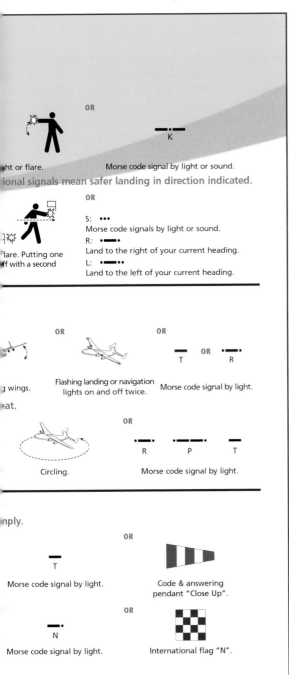

OR

K

...ght or flare.   Morse code signal by light or sound.

...ional signals mean safer landing in direction indicated.

OR

S: •••
Morse code signals by light or sound.
R: •—•
Land to the right of your current heading.
L: •—••
Land to the left of your current heading.

...lare. Putting one
...ff with a second

OR   OR

T   R

Morse code signal by light.

...g wings.   Flashing landing or navigation lights on and off twice.   Morse code signal by light.

...at.

OR

R   P   T

Circling.   Morse code signal by light.

...ply.

OR

T

Morse code signal by light.   Code & answering pendant "Close Up".

OR

N

Morse code signal by light.   International flag "N".

Flares and a waterproof container.

made to the Coastguard as soon as possible. If another vessel requires assistance it must be provided, if it is safe and reasonable to do so.

4 Misuse of distress flares

It is illegal and irresponsible to let off distress signals if you are not in distress, even at a bonfire party. All sightings of flares that are reported to the Coastguard by radio or phone are investigated, so resources could be diverted from a genuine emergency. Once flares pass their expiry date they can be handed in to a Coastguard station for safe disposal. Do not throw old flares over the side, throw them out with the rubbish or bury them in the garden!

- If you are planning a foreign trip then it is important to check local regulations, which tend to be far more complicated and restrictive. For RYA* members there are excellent booklets and abundant advice available from the Cruising Department. For some countries the skipper or all the helmsmen may need the International Certificate of Competence (ICC). This is not difficult and not too expensive to sort out. Again contact the RYA*, this time the Training Division, or a local sea school for advice.

Passage planning: 2
The navigation plan

Passage planning is quite fun, rather like poring over holiday brochures deciding on the next trip. With a day sail from your own marina or mooring the plan may consist of checking the tides, looking at the forecast and saying to the family "Let's go, the weather and the tides are right. We can be there in time to have a picnic lunch and be back before dark. I have told Grandma we will call in on the way home at about 8 o'clock. If it gets late we'll motor back."

That is a passage plan because it considers some of the most important aspects including:

- Is the weather ok?
- Are the tides right?
- Will there be enough water to get into the river or marina?
- Will the tidal streams help or hinder the trip?
- Is the trip suitable for the boat and the crew?
- What is the contingency plan if it gets dark, the weather deteriorates or something else goes wrong?
- Does someone else know of our plan?

For a more complicated passage more detailed planning is necessary because of the regulations and for an enjoyable trip.

Look at the three different phases of the trip when you start the plan:

PHASE ONE Getting out	PHASE TWO Getting there	PHASE THREE Getting in

People often ask which of the three phases is the most important and which will determine when we go, but that is hard to say initially. In some cases when the boat arrives is so critical that the passage will be planned back from that, but make no firm decisions too quickly. Look at all three phases, then firm up the plan.

Getting out / getting in
The first and last phases of the journey have many similar potential problems:

- What is the **charted depth**? If there is not enough water to get in and out at all states of the tide then calculate the **earliest** and the **latest** time that you will be able to leave and arrive. It is ideal to be crossing shallow areas on a rising tide, if possible.
- Is it possible to enter or leave in the **dark**? Are there enough lit buoys to do this and are you comfortable with the idea? If you have never been to a port before, making the first entry at night could be very stressful. Check sunrise or sunset times in the almanac.
- Will a strong **tidal stream** in a narrow channel make entering or leaving difficult or even impossible?
- Plan the **pilotage** into and out of rivers and harbours. Check in the almanac for the opening times of any **lock** or **bridge**.
- Check the local **regulations** and practices for traffic signals, calling for permission to leave or enter on VHF, monitoring VHF for shipping movements, use of the engine, hours when the office or water taxi will be manned.
- What **hazards** can you expect? It may be necessary to look out for commercial

shipping, fishing boats, fishing pots, areas of moorings or unlit buoys.

- The skipper of a motor cruiser needs to check on the availability of **fuel** for the outward and return passages.
- At the end of the journey there needs to be a **'what if'** plan built in. What if we arrive early or late so that it is too dark or too shallow to get into the planned marina or harbour? Calculate the latest time that the boat will be able to go in and then plan what to do if you're late. It may mean going to another port altogether, picking up a mooring, anchoring or just waiting for more light or more height of tide.

This part of the planning may show up problems, but it may be possible to work round them. Examples:

1. The best time to leave to catch the tidal stream down the coast does not fit in with the opening of a lock gate. So exit the lock, pick up a mooring, or anchor and wait for the tidal stream to be favourable. This will avoid the problem of being with the tidal stream for an hour through the lock and down the river, then against it for the rest of the day.

2. It may be necessary to leave the river during daylight when the tidal streams are wrong for the passage. So come out of the river the day before, stop overnight at the nearest convenient anchorage or mooring, then make the passage.

3. The time to go into the shallow harbour does not fit with the tidal stream down the coast to get there. So make best use of the tidal streams and check the chart for somewhere to moor and wait to go in.

Getting there

The middle phase of the planning usually takes longer, and may seem more complicated as it will often be necessary to use several charts. When on passage it is important to use detailed charts, especially near the coast or other hazards, but for the initial plan a chart which shows the whole route is useful too.

Look in detail at the following:

- **How far** is it and, at the average speed of the boat, about **how long** should it take to get there? The first ETA will always be very approximate. The tidal streams hopefully can be with the boat on a coastal passage and therefore increase the speed over the ground. With a yacht there can be a problem with **wind direction** on the day. A yacht tacking, that is sailing against the wind, but with the tidal stream, will have to sail about half as far again to get to the destination. Bad, but not as bad as sailing against the tidal stream and against the wind when the boat will have to sail about twice as far. This means that to achieve 10 miles towards the destination the boat will have to sail approximately 20 miles. This can be very demoralising for all on board and is best avoided!
- **Tidal streams.** When will they be favourable? For a coastal passage this may be the most important factor in the plan and make when to leave as obvious as looking up a train timetable. Make up the tidal stream atlas in real time for the day, then it is easy to see when the tidal streams become favourable and, just as important, when they turn against the boat.
  Tidal streams tend to flow along the coast so their influence will be much more important at the planning stage if the passage is up or down the coast, especially for a yacht.
  On a yacht where the average speed is 5 or 6 knots it makes sense to **sail**

with the tidal steams, as the speed over the ground will be greater and the journey time reduced. It may be possible to add up the average speeds of the tidal streams for each hour and so estimate the time saving, to improve the initial ETA. For a planing motor cruiser a more important factor may be **sea state**. The sea will be smoother when the wind and the tidal stream are in the same direction. Smooth conditions make it possible to maintain the optimum cruising speed for fuel efficiency and a pleasant trip.

- **Plan the Route.** It is useful to have a chart that shows the whole journey as on that scale the general direction and distance can be seen. If this is not possible then draw a sketch map and write the details of distances and directions on that. Check the route on the detailed charts to be used on the passage, to be sure that it is safe. Drawing the route gives the opportunity to select the waypoints and measure the distances and directions between them. If these waypoints are going to be used as a route in the GPS it is vital that the distances and directions measured from the chart are checked against those calculated by the GPS. Putting waypoints into the GPS incorrectly is extremely easy to do, and can be very dangerous. Skippers of fast boats often place the waypoints near the buoys rather than on them!

- What **hazards** are there to avoid along the route such as sandbanks, rocks, traffic separation schemes or areas busy with commercial shipping or fishing boats?

- Look on the route for any **tidal gates**. These are points on the route where the tidal stream is particularly critical. Round a headland the tidal streams can be exceptionally strong making it important not to be late.

Look at the plan as whole:
Look at all three phases of the passage to find the best way of fitting them together.

Remember that if the arrival time is critical but the wind is very light the skipper and crew of a sailing boat may have to use the engine to arrive on time or not go at all. A passage is a journey like any other and once the timetable has been planned it must be adhered to, or the destination changed.

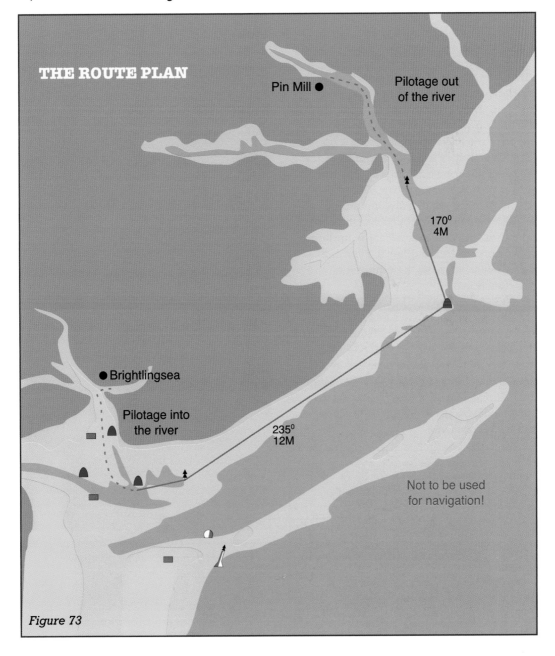

THE ROUTE PLAN

Pin Mill ●

Pilotage out
of the river

170⁰
4M

● Brightlingsea

Pilotage into
the river

235⁰
12M

Not to be used
for navigation!

Figure 73

Looking at electronics: 1 The basics

When you buy or charter a boat it will probably come stuffed with electronic gadgets. They are a great boon, but if you are buying your own there are lots to choose from and expert advice is a good idea. Even better is the opportunity to try them out afloat on a friend's boat, a sailing school boat or a charter trip. Things to consider are not just the immediate benefits and the initial costs but the ease of operation, the size of screen, the updating requirements and whether the use can be extended to make the equipment multifunctional.

The navigator's most basic tool after the steering compass is the **log**, which measures the distance travelled and the speed through the water. Most logs these days use a paddlewheel transducer mounted through the hull. The display needs to be easy to read and the information available to the navigator and the helmsman.

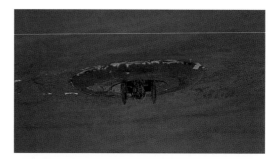

The paddlewheel of the log transducer projects below the hull (top). It can be withdrawn for cleaning (below).

A multi display.
The log shows we have sailed 15 miles.

The **log transducer** is vulnerable to fouling by weed, but can easily be cleaned by withdrawing it through the hull. This is quite safe, even when the boat is in the water, as the opening will be protected by a flap

The depth is 10.1 metres.

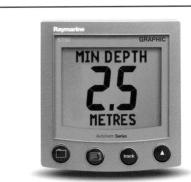

Set the shallow water alarm to something you are comfortable with e.g. 2.5 metres.

hand over the opening will stop the water coming in but makes the maintenance job very difficult! I have found a large sponge pushed well into the hole works well, but this is only very temporary and obviously needs to be watched carefully. If the paddlewheel is not clean the log will probably under-read, which will be confusing and perhaps dangerous. The accuracy can be checked over a measured distance and then the instrument calibrated to read correctly. Don't forget about the tidal streams if you try this and use slack water if possible or do two runs, one with the tide and one against. If a second-hand instrument is persistently giving trouble, even when the transducer is clean, it is probably best to have the installation checked profes-sionally, as any replacement transducer needs to be compatible with the instrument. Alternatively the GPS can be used to help calibrate the log.

The modern digital **echosounder** is easy to read and will include features such as shallow water and deep water alarms, which can be very useful in pilotage situations. Some people think that the purpose of an echosounder is to stop a boat going aground. This is obviously not so, as boats seem to go aground all over

warning that the boat is out of a channel, not so that there is a split second warning before the bump. The deep water alarm can be useful in avoiding a big ship channel. Usually the instrument can be set up to read depth below the transducer, depth beneath the keel or depth of the water. Decide which you think is best and if you go on other boats it is useful to know how it has been set up too.

Once the log and the echosounder are set up and working well, the next most important instrument is the **VHF/DSC** - not exactly for navigation, but an essential part of the electronic kit on a boat nevertheless. A handheld set has the advantage of being portable if you sail on lots of different boats,

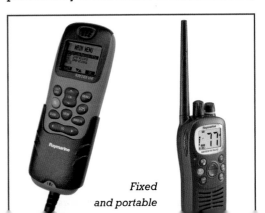

Fixed
and portable

but the low aerial, low power transmission and lack of DSC capability reduce its appeal for the owner of a boat. In the almanac will be found the VHF channels to monitor or use (if necessary) in harbour areas and the times of the Maritime Safety Information Broadcasts made by HM Coastguard. These broadcasts include weather forecasts and navigation warnings. While at sea skippers are advised to monitor channel 16. (Avoid transmitting on channel 16, except in an emergency.)

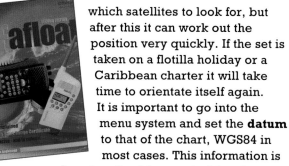

A GPS set giving your latitude and longitude.

The next instrument most navigators want is a **GPS**, in fact many buy a hand-held GPS before owning a boat because they are such a valuable aid to navigation. The basic sets, no bigger than a mobile phone, have an internal aerial and work off batteries so can be taken and used anywhere. Even these sets have many features beyond the position display, such as the ability to store waypoints, build a route, show directions as true or magnetic, change datum and many more. When first switched on in a new location the set has to work quite hard to calculate where in the world it is and therefore

which satellites to look for, but after this it can work out the position very quickly. If the set is taken on a flotilla holiday or a Caribbean charter it will take time to orientate itself again. It is important to go into the menu system and set the **datum** to that of the chart, WGS84 in most cases. This information is found on the title panel of the chart.

For the boat owner there are advantages in having a bigger built-in set connected to the boat's power supply and with a fixed external aerial. The position from this set can be interfaced via an NMEA connection to the VHF/DSC set, and to other equipment such as an electronic chart plotter, Yeoman plotter or radar set. The GPS needs an aerial that can 'see the sky' and it should be mounted low down on the boat for the best signal quality.

The **Yeoman plotter** is another aid to consider. This British invention has been around for a few years but continual developments during that time mean that it has a lot to offer at a relatively low price. It provides **a link between the paper chart and the GPS**, to eliminate the most common mistakes. Any chart can be used with the active mat on the chart table, with the A2 folio charts from the Admiralty, Imray or Stanfords fitting perfectly. The chart can be held in place and protected by a soft plastic cover. All the plotting can be done on this cover with the chart seen perfectly through it. The link to the GPS and the active mat is made by a special sort of computer mouse, called a puck. Every time the chart is changed it has to be referenced to the plotter, and then the position from the GPS can be transferred to the chart in seconds, error free. A waypoint can be stored in the GPS at the press of a button with no possibility of a mistake.

The puck can be used to measure distances and directions, and with practice any of the plotting normally done with a Breton-type plotter can be done with it. The Yeoman is robust, protects the paper chart, and can be updated by buying a new folio of paper charts - but best of all it helps prevent the most common plotting errors, mistakes transferring latitude and longitude from the chart to the GPS and the GPS to the chart. The Yeoman is quick and easy to use with very little practise and its usefulness seems to grow the longer you have it on the boat. Where there is no chart table on the boat a portable version can be used which includes a rigid board and cover.

More information from www.precisionnavigation.co.uk.

Looking at Electronics: 2 Chartplotters

Chartplotters are a more recent development and they are becoming increasingly popular. They are not a substitute for understanding navigation or the ability to navigate at sea, just a different way of doing it. They use a screen to display the electronic chart and are combined or interfaced with a GPS set to show the boat's position, updating as it moves. Things are changing very rapidly with this technology and it is potentially very expensive so get advice from experts, as there are several options

to choose from. Some plotters have stored tidal data and can calculate a course to steer as well, so they form a complete navigation system.

The basic requirements are:

• **A screen** on which to display the electronic charts. This can be a computer screen, which means taking a laptop afloat, or a dedicated chartplotter. The plotter may have a much smaller screen, indeed some

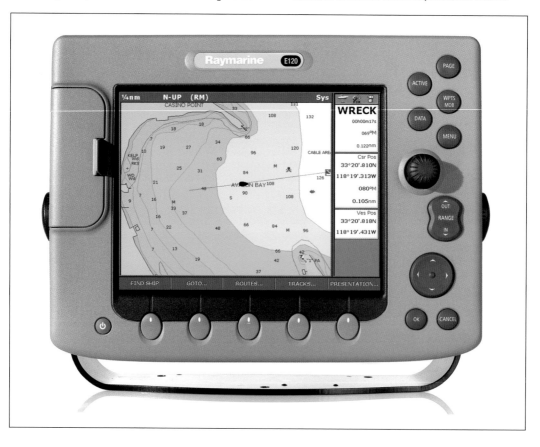

are very small but, unlike the computer, it will have been manufactured for the marine environment, by marine specialists.

- **The software** to make the charts work. The plotter will include the software within it but a computer will require additional software before it can run the charts, except in the case of the Admiralty RYA* Electronic Chart Plotter. The computer software tends to be more complex to operate, but once the computer system is in place on the boat it can be used for many additional tasks such as connecting to the internet, long range communication and obtaining weather information. A computer-driven system is popular with skippers doing extended cruising.

- **The electronic charts** themselves have to be bought to use on the computer screen or plotter. The charts come in two different types, **raster** and **vector**. The way the chart image is produced on the screen is different, giving the charts different characteristics in use. The other important considerations are the source of the data used to compile the charts, the updating facility and its cost. Remember that the UKHO, who are an agency of the government, publish chart corrections weekly to an international standard for paper charts but that will not be true for all producers of electronic charts. Charts can become out of date very quickly.

The raster chart, or raster scan chart to give it the full name, is a scanned version of a paper chart, so it looks exactly the same. These are the ones most commonly used on computers. The UKHO produce ARCS charts, the Admiralty Raster Chart System, on CDs for displaying on computer screens with the use of additional software. The ARCS Skipper

* denotes a trademark registered by the RYA.

Service is the leisure version of their chart system used by ships. The charts can be bought individually or in folios of 10 and there is chart coverage of the world. Once purchased, an electronic chart requires updating like any other and this is by CD also. The UKHO provides a very regular and reliable service for this, just as it does for paper charts, but it is an additional cost.

The scanned charts produce a picture on the screen that is very familiar, but like any scanned image it cannot be changed or manipulated in any way. There is no information beyond what is on the chart. The picture is built up on the screen by illuminating pixels, like an LCD screen, and these produce a very distorted picture if zoomed beyond their natural scale.

In 2004 the UKHO produced the Admiralty RYA* Electronic Chart Plotter in conjunction with the RYA* Training Division. This is a stand-alone CD holding 15 charts for local areas. Additional software to operate these charts is not required and this provides an excellent and inexpensive way of trying out the idea of electronic charts. It can be used at home to place waypoints and form a route as part of a passage plan, and then afloat on a laptop to navigate at sea. The computer can receive GPS input and then will display the vessel's position on the chart, updating it as the boat moves. The GPS information can be from a handheld GPS, a built-in set or from an active aerial, known as a GPS engine. The GPS engine is an aerial with no screen and the GPS position is fed directly to other electronic equipment. The CD is licensed for a year, so to update the charts it is necessary to buy a new disc, because it will stop working! No chance of using out-of-date charts here.

A training version of this plotter, using the RYA* training charts, is used on all RYA* shorebased courses and is supplied to the students with their course packs. Additionally it can be bought separately from the RYA*. It includes a booklet with instructions and an audio commentary by Tom Cunliffe.

Vector charts are produced by a completely different and more complicated system. The picture is built up from layers of information, so the image on the screen can be changed. The software to run the chart is in the dedicated plotter and it can manipulate the image to different scales. You can, for example, omit some data or interrogate a buoy for more information. This versatility has led to vector charts being called intelligent charts. Many consider that vector charts are the way ahead for all navigation systems. They are the newest and fastest developing technology.

Other possibilities include setting alarms to warn of hazards and shallow water. The menu systems of plotters tend to be less complicated too and the controls easier to use at sea than a computer. The unit will also be waterproof, robust and fixed in position, unlike a computer that is used on board occasionally. Additionally, if there is a problem with the plotter then there is one manufacturer to deal with - not three as in the case of a computer manufacturer, software company and chart producer.

The source of the data for vector charts may be commercial companies not government agencies so check how up-to-date the charts will be when you buy them and the updating facilities.

No chart plotting system can be seen as a single purchase. Paper charts get damaged with use and wear so we have to buy more, while those on a screen remain pristine. Don't be fooled: they require updating too. Out-of-date charts or those produced with low quality data will lead to uncertainty and possibly to danger.

Even with good quality, up-to-date electronic charts on board and the ability to use them, carry sufficient paper charts and practise plotting skills because electronics or their power supply do occasionally fail. And anyway, navigation is fun!

Zooming in on a vector chart for more detail.

Sierra
... the passage continued

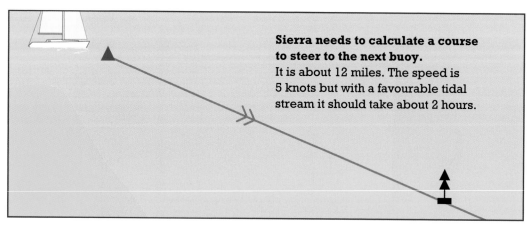

Sierra needs to calculate a course to steer to the next buoy.
It is about 12 miles. The speed is 5 knots but with a favourable tidal stream it should take about 2 hours.

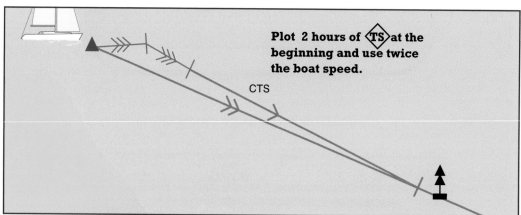

Plot 2 hours of ⟨TS⟩ at the beginning and use twice the boat speed.

CTS

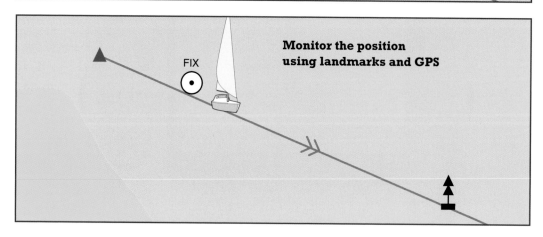

Monitor the position using landmarks and GPS

FIX

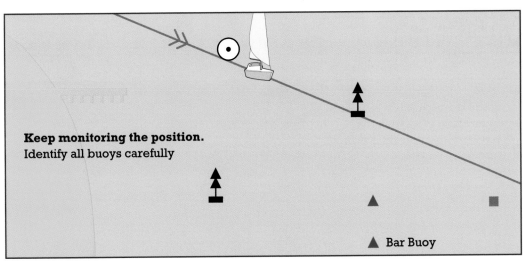

Keep monitoring the position.
Identify all buoys carefully

▲ Bar Buoy

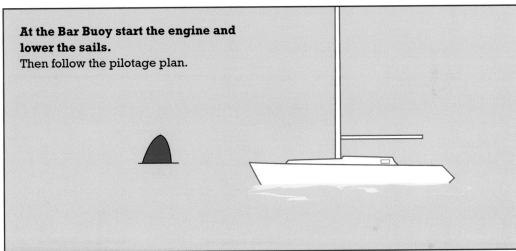

At the Bar Buoy start the engine and lower the sails.
Then follow the pilotage plan.

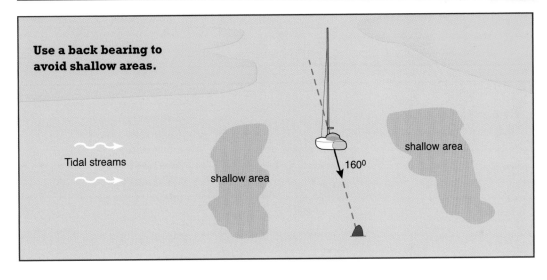

Use a back bearing to avoid shallow areas.

Tidal streams

shallow area

shallow area

160⁰

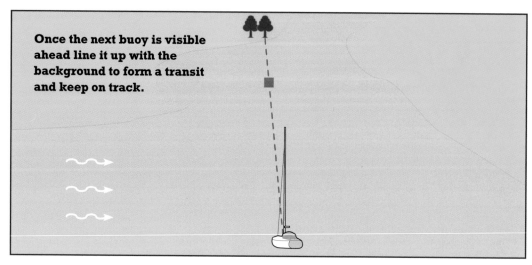

Once the next buoy is visible ahead line it up with the background to form a transit and keep on track.

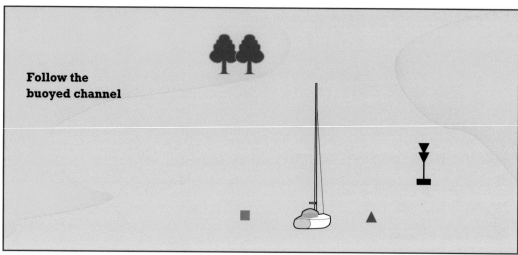

Follow the buoyed channel

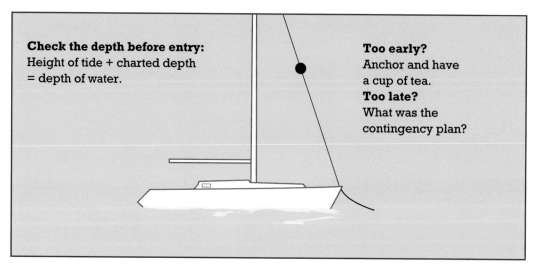

Check the depth before entry:
Height of tide + charted depth = depth of water.

Too early?
Anchor and have a cup of tea.
Too late?
What was the contingency plan?

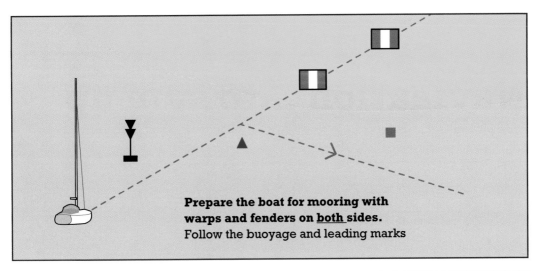

Prepare the boat for mooring with warps and fenders on <u>both</u> sides.
Follow the buoyage and leading marks

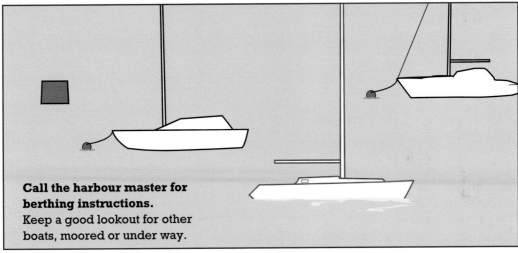

Call the harbour master for berthing instructions.
Keep a good lookout for other boats, moored or under way.

Moor up. Tidy the boat, then put the kettle on and relax... and plan your next voyage!

Navigation ...to sum up

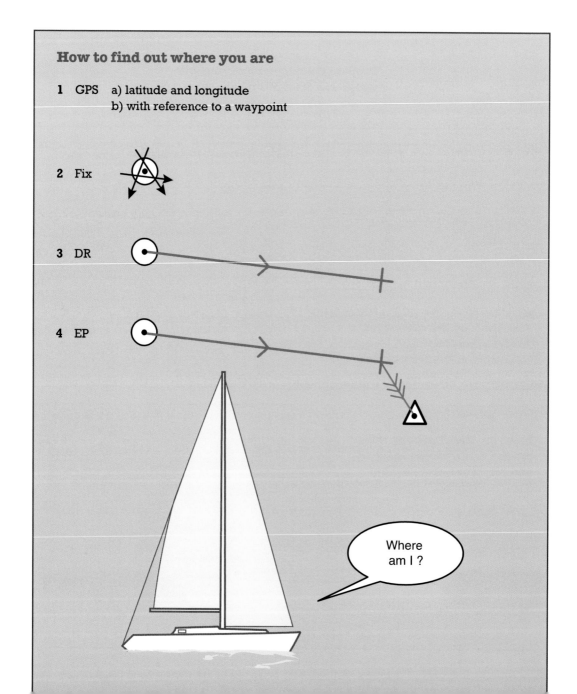

How to find the place you want to get to

1   CTS

How do I get
to the next point?

Thats all there

is to it!

Glossary

COG. The Course Over the Ground or ground track. Shown on the chart with 2 arrows. It is the path over the seabed that the boat has travelled or will travel along.

Chart datum. Chart datum is the level used on the charts to show the charted depth. It is approximately the Lowest Astronomical Tide.

CTS. A course to steer is a course calculated in advance to allow for the predicted tidal streams and the estimated leeway.

Depth of water. The depth of water is a combination of the height of tide and the charted depth or drying height shown on the chart.

Deviation. This is caused by the boat's magnetic field, and affects each compass differently, depending on its position on the boat. It also varies with the boat's heading.

DR. A position based only on the distance and direction sailed through the water. Leeway may be allowed for. A very basic position.

EP. A estimated position is a DR position with the tidal stream taken into account and plotted.

Height of tide. The height of tide is the amount of water above chart datum. The figures in tide tables are the height of tide at HW and LW. In between HW and LW height of tide can be calculated using the tidal curve diagram.

Interpolate. Insert a number in a series so it fits the sequence. E.g. a number one-sixth of the way between 12 and 24 is 14.

SOG. The speed over the ground is **not** shown on the log. SOG is the combination of the speed through the water (shown on the log) and the tidal stream. It can be shown on a GPS.

TTG. Time to go. When added to the current time, gives the ETA.

Variation. Variation applies to both steering and hand-bearing compasses and is caused by the world's magnetic field. It is the difference between the magnetic reading on the compass and the chart (the chart is drawn to true north). Variation is different in different places in the world and the information for a location is found on the compass rose.

Waypoint. A waypoint is a point on the chart chosen by the navigator. It can be any point or a buoy used as part of a route. If the latitude and longitude of this waypoint are put into the GPS, the set will display the direction and distance **to** the waypoint, updated as the boat moves. The original purpose of the waypoint feature was as part of a route, but it can also be used to make plotting your position quicker and easier than using latitude and longitude.

XTE. Cross Track Error. When a waypoint is put into the GPS the set will show the direction and distance to the waypoint, updating as the boat moves. The XTE is the distance, in tenths of a mile, that the boat has been pushed off the original direction given by the GPS.

Websites.
www.rya.org.uk
www.mcga.gov.uk
www.ukho.gov.uk
www.fernhurstbooks.co.uk
www.pinmillcruising.co.uk
www.raymarine.com